CW01310100

OLYSLAGER AUTO LIBRARY

American Cars of the 1960s

compiled by the OLYSLAGER ORGANISATION

FREDERICK WARNE
London and New York

THE OLYSLAGER AUTO LIBRARY

This book is one of a growing range of titles on major transport subjects.
Titles published so far include:

The Jeep
Cross-Country Cars from 1945
Half-Tracks
Scammell Vehicles
Tanks and Transport Vehicles of World War 2
Armour on Wheels to 1942
Fire-Fighting Vehicles 1840–1950
Fire and Crash Vehicles from 1950
Earthmoving Vehicles
Wreckers and Recovery Vehicles
Passenger Vehicles 1893–1940
Buses and Coaches from 1940
Fairground and Circus Transport

American Cars of the 1930s
American Cars of the 1940s
American Cars of the 1950s
American Cars of the 1960s
American Trucks of the Early Thirties
American Trucks of the Late Thirties

British Cars of the Early Thirties
British Cars of the Late Thirties
British Cars of the Early Forties
British Cars of the Late Forties
British Cars of the Early Fifties
British Cars of the Late Fifties

Motorcycles to 1945
Motorcycles and Scooters from 1945

Copyright © Olyslager Organisation BV 1977

First published 1977 by Frederick Warne (Publishers) Ltd, London

Reprinted 1978, 1979

ISBN 0 7232 2061 1

Filmset and printed in Great Britain
by BAS Printers Limited, Over Wallop, Hampshire
D5985.679

INTRODUCTION

This volume, like the preceding books of *American Cars of the 1930s*, *American Cars of the 1940s* and *American Cars of the 1950s* is set out on a year-by-year basis, covering cars produced in North America during the period of 1960-69. The nineteen-sixties was the decade in which the future dream car of the fifties had to become a reality. It did and yet, it did not.

As never before, the sales of imported cars rose to a disconcerting level, with VW's Beetle in the lead.

Few left-overs from the late fifties styling experiments disrupted the early sixties model fashion producing huge tail fins and over-decorated, over-ornamented battleships. At the same time, however, the compact car was born, the Big Three each launching their own version almost simultaneously: GM's Chevrolet Corvair, by far the most interesting with its air-cooled, rear-mounted 'flat-six', Chrysler's fashionable Valiant and Ford's rather dull-looking Falcon. From then on, the compact car grew until the original idea seemed to have been forgotten by the public and the Big Three introduced intermediate versions that were slightly larger.

American Motors Corporation, as a small car manufacturer, suffered enormous losses when the buying public went 'full-size' again—but managed to survive. This was not the case, however, with the unfortunate Studebaker which finally lost the struggle in 1966. Even their move from South Bend in Indiana in 1964 to their Canadian Hamilton factory did not help. Their latest brain child, the Avanti, still lives as a separate make to this day.

Along with technical sophistication such as a growing amount of automatic transmissions, air-conditioning, power brakes, power steering, front disc brakes and alternators, the sixties were marked by a growing safety consciousness. This was inspired in no small way by Ralph Nader and his book *Unsafe at Any Speed*. It finally broke down the Chevrolet Corvair, but it also severely affected VW Beetle sales.

The front-wheel driven Eldorado and Toronado from General Motors also surprised the World. Front-wheel drive on production cars had not been used in America since before the Second World War.

Replicas like the Excalibur and the Cord hit the road in the mid-sixties, though the Cord project died within a year.

A sales record of ten million cars and trucks was hit in 1965, but the general economic situation caused a drop until 1968, when once again sales improved.

American Motors made an effort by penetrating into the European market on two different occasions and with two completely different cars: firstly with the Metropolitan from 1960–62 and secondly with the Rambler Renault from 1963–67. The first car was an Austin-based two-plus-two, the latter a CKD project, the cars being built at the Austin Longbridge plant and the Belgian Renault factory respectively.

Towards the end of the decade a good many sports saloons had found their niche in the market such as the Javelin, Avanti II, sporty Comets and Falcons, Marlin, Camaro and the immensely successful Corvette, Ford Mustang, Thunderbird and others.

The dream car had become a reality. Towards the seventies, the American car, although still a big car by any standard, somehow managed to look as if a lot more commonsense had been built into it than ever before. The dream car will never live!

Dick Schornagel

ABBREVIATIONS

AMC	American Motors Corporation
auto. trans.	automatic transmission
bhp	brake horsepower*
CID	cubic inch displacement, piston displacement in cubic inches
cu. in.	cubic inch (1 cu. in. = 16·39 cc)
CR	compression ratio
diff.	differential
Eight	eight cylinder (engine)
F-head	inlet-over-exhaust-valve (engine)
FWD	front wheel drive
GM	General Motors (Corporation)
IFS	independent front suspension
IRS	independent rear suspension
in.	inch (=2·54 cm)
L-head	side-valve engine
OHV	overhead valves
PAB	power-assisted brakes
PAS	power-assisted steering
RHD	right-hand drive
rpm	revolutions per minute
SAE	Society of Automotive Engineers
Six	six-cylinder in line (engine)
swb	short-wheelbase
V8	eight-cylinder in V-form (engine)
wb	wheelbase (distance between front and rear wheel centres)

*Until recently US manufacturers quoted gross bhp figures to SAE standards; these are used throughout the book where applicable. They are higher than the actual output of the engine as installed in the vehicle.

1960 The total passenger car sales for 1960 were 6,641,000—over a million more than during the previous year. In the late fifties, US cars featured the most extravagant body styling of all times. Huge tail fins, wrap around rear windows and, in most cases, over-decoration in chrome ornaments, front grilles and hub caps. The 1960s, however, commenced encouragingly with the first 'compacts', though the heritage of the styling in the past decade was still obvious in the new model year. US car sales in the previous decade, 1950 to 1959, amounted to 69,400,000 vehicles. Imports were rising steeply with the Volkswagen Beetle from Europe as an unbeatable number one. Predictions for the 1960s were a sales figure of 150,000,000 US cars. The Ford Edsel line was dropped in November 1959, though a revised 1960 model had already been launched. General Motors, Chrysler and Ford introduced their all new Corvair, Valiant and Falcon compacts. The rear-engined Corvair with its air-cooled flat six power plant was the most interesting entrant in this field. Chevrolet at the same time was having difficulty with its aluminium heads, initially meant for the 283 CID Corvette. They tended to crack around the stud bosses. The aluminium head was to come, but the big three were still working on it in 1960.

4A Buick Invicta 4600

4B Cadillac Sixty-Two Sedan

4A: Buick Invicta 4600, Model 4637. New grille and smaller tail fins on an otherwise very slightly modified body for 1960. Buick utilized two V-8 engines only: the Wildcat 384 for Le Sabre models and the bigger Wildcat 445 version for the Invicta and Electra series. A 3-speed manual gearbox was available as standard with an automatic transmission as an optional extra. Body styles offered were a 2-door and a 4-door Hardtop, a 2-door Convertible and a 4-door Hardtop Electra, with an extended rear deck for representation purposes.

4B: Cadillac 62 Series, Model 6338E. This 6-window Sedan, as opposed to the 4-window Sedan de Ville which featured the curved rear screen, as on Chevrolet's Impala of the period, showed clean, uncluttered lines with lower tail fins and less decoration than in the previous year. Built on a 130-in. wheelbase, all models except the series Seventy-Five measured 225 in. in length. Cadillac offered two V-8 engines for 1960, one with a four-barrel carb design and one with three dual-barrel carbs, the latter being a standard fitting on Eldorado, Biarritz, Seville and Brougham models.

4C: Chevrolet Corvair 500 Sedan, GM's first compact, rear-engined 'Beetle-eater' cost $2100 in its first year, while the Beetle was still only $1550! There were two models: Standard 500 and de Luxe 700, and only one engine. In February the Monza Coupé model joined the range. The 'Turbo-Air' was a pushrod operated OHV horizontally opposed Six, air-cooled, with 2 single-barrel carbs. Floor-operated 3-speed manual with non-synchromesh first gear. Powerglide automatic transmission was an option. Drum brakes front and rear. No separate chassis, but a welded unit construction with independent suspension all round. Wheelbase 108 in.; overall length 180 in.

4C Chevrolet Corvair 500 Sedan

5A Chevrolet Corvette XP-700

5B Chevrolet Impala Convertible

5C Chrysler Valiant V-200

5D DeSoto Adventurer 2-door Hardtop

5E Dodge Dart Phoenix

5A: Chevrolet Corvette XP-700. Experimental fibre-glass body sharing Corvette's techniques. The XP-700 looked as though it should be orbiting the earth. Chief General Motors stylist William (Bill) L. Mitchell took credit for the design. The XP-700 was 48 in. high, 4 in. lower even than the production body. Note periscope rear view mirror. Only one prototype was built.

5B: Chevrolet Impala Convertible, Model 1867E. Top of Impala line, featured six-in-line or V-8 engines and manual 3-speed or Powerglide automatic transmission. For the whole 1960 range, except the Corvair, a choice of seven engines and five transmissions was offered: the Hi-Thrift 6 in three versions, the Turbo-Fire V-8 using regular fuel. and the hotter versions Super Turbo-Fire V-8 230 bhp, Turbo-Thrust V-8 250 bhp and Super Turbo-Thrust V-8 of 280 bhp. The transmissions were the 3-speed synchromesh, the top-economy overdrive, 4-speed synchromesh, Powerglide and Turboglide automatic for 6- and 8-cylinder models. This, coupled with a choice of four Impala models, seven Bel-Airs, three bottom of the line Biscayne, and five Wagons, gave an almost endless range of over 90 regular Chevrolets for 1960.

5C: Chrysler Valiant V-200 4-door Sedan. The all-new Compact from Chrysler was offered in two 4-door Sedan versions, the V-100 and V-200, as well as in two Wagon models, also the V-100 and V-200. Only one engine, the front-mounted 30 degrees inclined six-in-line of 170 CID (2780 cc), was available with a choice of two transmissions: one manual 3-speed floorshift and a 3-speed push-button control automatic transmission. Front suspension by torsion bars, at the rear a live axle and leaf springs. Typical model characteristics were a square 'European type' front grille and a fake spare wheel cover on the boot lid.

5D: DeSoto Adventurer, biggest model of the DeSoto line. Unit construction. Power option: Ram Charge engine with special inlet manifold, creating a compressor-like effect. The other series was named Fireflite.

5E: Dodge Dart Phoenix 4-door Hardtop, Model PD4-H-43. DeSoto was phased out in 1960, still leaving the Chrysler Corporation with four models of large cars of which, apart from the new Valiant Compact, the Dodge Dart then became the bottom of the line model. Darts, based on a 118-in. wheelbase, were available in these series, totalling 26 models: the basic Seneca, the Pioneer and the top of the line Phoenix, with a choice of a new 6-cylinder OHV-engine of 225 CID and two V-8 power units of 318 and 383 CID respectively. Standard transmission was a manual 3-speed synchromesh, while two automatic transmissions, the Powerflite 2-speed and the Torqueflite 3-speed were available at extra cost.

1960

6A: Ford Falcon 4-door Sedan. Powered by a 90 hp in-line 6 of 144·3 CID, the new Falcon featured a unit construction body with IFS and a live rear axle with semi-elliptic leaf springs. Manual 3-speed (column shift) lacked synchromesh on first; 2-speed automatic transmission was an option at extra cost. Ford Falcon came in two body styles, 2- and 4-door sedans. Prices started from $1912, so were slightly lower than both Corvair and Valiant, though still $362 over the top-selling VW Beetle. Wheelbase was 109·5 in.; overall length 181·1 in. Boosted in advertisements as a full 6-seater, all three new compact cars were no more than just 4-seaters, the Falcon being the roomiest, if only marginally so.

6B: Ford Galaxie was top of the range of the regulars. Technically based on the Fairlanes, the Galaxie had the 'Thunderbird look', emphasized by the roof line. Thunderbird engines were available for this model. Note unusual RHD (for British market).

6C: Ford Thunderbird was called 'America's most wanted car' and for 1960 featured a completely automatic convertible top, which at the touch of a button folded down under the rear deck lid into the luggage compartment. There was also a Hardtop version and two V-8 engine options: the 300 hp 352 Special and the 350 hp 430 Special, the latter with pre-heated carburettor air induction system and in-block wedge-type combustion chambers. Available with Cruise-O-Matic Drive only, whereas 352 engine had a choice of 3-speed, Overdrive and Cruise-O-Matic transmissions.

6D: Imperial Le Baron Model PY1-H. In this prestige model of the Chrysler Company, the full treatment of tail fins and over-decoration on body and interior styling is apparent. Available with one 413 CID V-8 power plant and Torque-Flite automatic transmission only. IFS, torsion bar springs, live rear axle, tapered-leaf outboard rear springs with interliners and rear axle strut. Other Imperial models were Imperial Custom 4-door Sedan, Custom 2-door Southampton, 2-door Crown, 4-door Crown Southampton, 4-door Crown Sedan, Crown Convertible and 4-door Le Baron Sedan.

6E: Lincoln Continental, built by Mercury, was Ford's most prestigious car and has been popular with many White House administrations. For 1960 a new Hotchkiss rear suspension with leaf springs was introduced. Another model was Lincoln Première. Body styles were Hardtop, Convertible, Limousine and Formal Sedan.

6A Ford Falcon

6B Ford Galaxie Town Sedan

6C Ford Thunderbird

6D Imperial Le Baron

6E Lincoln Continental Mk. V

1960

7A: Mercury Comet, introduced in February, was designed with the chief aim of marketing a car that offered much more value in luxury features for just a little more money. The Mercury Comet was originally planned as a successor to the obsolete Ford Edsel. Falcon's big brother was just 1 ft longer. The same Falcon basic unit body with the same interior space was used, the floor pans were changed, the rear axle was moved back $4\frac{1}{2}$ in., the boot was enlarged and a different roof line was used. The front and rear wings were changed to identify it with the Mercury. The same Falcon 90-bhp OHV six-in-line engine was used.

7B: Mercury, as a separate Ford Division, offered three series for 1960: Monterey, Montclair and Park Lane, plus three engine options (V-8), ranging from 208 Economy to the 314-bhp Marauder. Three-speed manual transmission in conjunction with 208-bhp engine only; Merc-O-Matic or Multi-Drive automatic transmission available with all engine options, though Multi-Drive was not available with 208 hp engine. For 1960 Mercury introduced 'Road-Tuned' wheels, which meant the body stayed level while wheels and suspension coped with road shocks.

7C: Metropolitan was an American Motors-designed body on an Austin chassis, powered by an existing 1500 cc 4-cylinder Austin engine. Some minor differences were, for instance, a Zenith downdraft carburettor instead of the normally fitted SU and a mechanical fuel pump. The car was also marketed outside the United States during certain periods, and several improvements were undertaken until the project finally died in 1961. There was a Convertible and a Hardtop model only.

7D: Oldsmobile Dynamic '88' Model 3539-D. Using the same body style as Chevrolet and Pontiac of that year, Oldsmobile retained distinctive front and rear-end styling, featuring two lines ('88' and '98'), five different body styles and basically one V-8 engine in two versions: Regular Rocket and Premium Rocket. Transmission options included 3-speed synchromesh as standard on Dynamic 88 and Super 88, and Jetaway Hydramatic Drive standard on '98' series, and optional on other series. Ninety-Eight Series had a 3·3-in. longer wheelbase.

7E: Plymouth Fury 8 Model PP2-H. One of 23 models in three Plymouth ranges. For 1960 Plymouth used unitary construction for their cars instead of separate chassis. Note the pomposity in styling and decor, coupled with enormous tail fins and the use of masses of chrome. The sales figures for 1960 Plymouth models were hardly successful!

7A Mercury Comet

7B Mercury Montclair Hardtop

7C Metropolitan 1500

7D Oldsmobile Dynamic '88' Sport Sedan

7E Plymouth Fury 8

1960

page 8

8A Pontiac Bonneville Sport Coupé

8A: Pontiac Bonneville Sport Coupé. This model shared the basic body shell with Chevrolet's Impala Coupé model. Note Vista-Panoramic windshield and low roof line. Pontiac's slightly boat-shaped front, typical for models yet to come, first became apparent in 1960. Pontiac still used X-frame chassis, IFS and live rear axle.

8B: Pontiac Laurentian 4-door Sedan Model 7519. As for the Bonneville, this model utilized the same Fisher body as used by Chevrolet. This particular model was built in GM's Canadian subsidiary. Other Pontiac 1960 models were: Catalina, Ventura, Star Chief for US market and Parisienne for Canadian market. A choice of nine varieties was offered.

8C: Rambler American once more encouraged the 'Big Three' to hurry with their compact models. Powered by a six-in-line engine, this relatively heavy car attained a top speed of just over 80 mph. New for 1960 was the 4-door Sedan.

8B Pontiac Laurentian

8C Rambler American

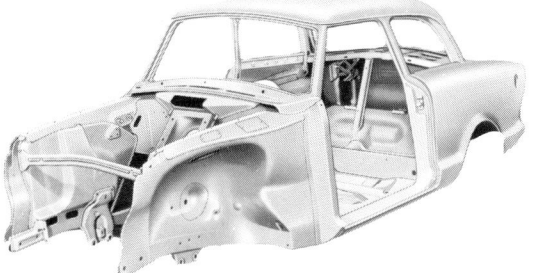

8D Single-unit body of Rambler American

8D: Rambler American's single-unit construction was made with more than 9000 welds to provide strength. This type of construction was used long before other US car makers followed suit.

1960

9A: Rambler Ambassador, though it had grown steadily, was still very much a Compact Car by US standards. The series incorporated a Super and a Custom Sedan and a 2-bench Station Wagon, plus a Custom hardtop Sedan and Station Wagon with 4 doors. The new Ambassador was powered by a V-8 engine which developed 250 bhp and operated on regular grade petrol. It shared the unitary body construction with the American series.

9A Rambler Ambassador

9B Studebaker Lark Convertible

9B: Studebaker Lark for 1960 was a European-sized vehicle with modest outer dimensions and appearance. It came in 2- and 4-door Sedan, 2-door Convertible and 4-door Station Wagon, with 6-cylinder and V-8 engines in top Regal line or with 6 or V-8 engine in De Luxe line. As with most US cars, the Lark was still based on an X-frame. Wheelbase for Sedans and Convertible was 108·5 in., for Wagon 113 in.

9C: Studebaker Hawk history dates back to 1953, in which year the Commander Regal Hardtop Coupé was introduced. The first Hawk though came in 1956, but the basic design was still available in 1960. Powered by either a six-in-line or a V-8 (90 and 180 bhp respectively!), these sporty 4-seater Coupés were of dynamic and almost timeless design. Overall length is 204 in.; wheelbase 120½ in.

9C Studebaker Hawk

1961

Car sales in 1961 were slightly down at 6,542,000 vehicles. Sales of the new compacts seemed to accelerate at first. Their number too had grown in the meantime and unlike most of the Big Three's regulars, which showed virtually no change in their basically 1958–60 chassis, the compacts like Dodge Lancer, Mercury Comet, Buick Special, Olds F-85 and Pontiac Tempest (the latter three sharing the same bodyshell) and the Buick and the Olds also the new aluminium V-8, were of a completely new design. It was the sheer concentration on basic engineering, unusual for a country where cars were sold mainly on their appearance, that marked 1961 as a year of technical progress. Of particular interest was Pontiac's 4-cylinder car—the Tempest. A design of very clean lines powered by an in-line 4, their own 390 CID cut in half and mounted at the front, but with a rear-mounted transmission and IRS. The Tempest's weight distribution was an ideal 50–50.

Suspension development in those days was aimed at a comfortable ride rather than better handling, although General Motors switched to coil springs at the rear, while Ford kept improving the age-old leaf-sprung Hotchkiss rear end.

The aluminium V-8 for Buick's Special and Oldsmobile's F-85 as well as the all-aluminium in-line 6 for the Rambler Classic, clearly marked another interesting new period in American engineering. The better weight distribution, too, gave the new compacts a better handling characteristic. At the same time automatic transmissions became fashionable and appeared as a standard feature on makes such as Cadillac, Continental, Ford Thunderbird and others.

Chrysler's make DeSoto was finally dropped on 20 December 1961. The first DeSoto came out in 1928.

10A Buick Special

10A: Buick Special was introduced in October 1963 and featured an all-aluminium V-8 engine of 215 CID, conventional front suspension and live rear axle. Two-speed automatic transmission was optional. Overall length 188·4 in.

10B: Buick Le Sabre, Model 4439E, was basic full-size model. Two others were Invicta and Electra. Two Wildcat V-8 engines, 238 bhp for Le Sabre and 319 bhp for the other series. Automatic transmission 'Turbine Drive' only.

10B Buick Le Sabre

10C: **Cadillac**, Model 6329E, gave a lower and sleeker impression than in the previous model year. The current series was 60, 62, 63 and 75—the latter model as a Limousine only.

10D: **Cadillac** 'Shaikh' was a $40,000 custom-built vehicle for His Highness Shaikh Abdullah Moobarrak Al-Sabah, the late ruler of the oil-rich kingdom of Kuwait. The car was armour-plated. The intended owner never used the car as he died before it was completed.

10C Cadillac Sedan de Ville

10D Cadillac 'Shaikh'

11A Chevrolet Corvair Lakewood Station Wagon

11C Chevrolet Greenbrier Sports Wagon

11A: **Chevrolet** Corvair Lakewood, Model 927B, was the third body style on the one-year-old Corvair. Owing to the rear-mounted engine, the floor was raised some 4 in., but in return for that it offered space in the front boot.

11B: **Chevrolet** Impala Sport Sedan, Model 1739, was one of six body styles and offered five engines and five transmission options. Note that tail fins had completely disappeared.

11C: **Chevrolet** Greenbrier Sports Wagon gave 9-passenger transport and was powered by a rear-mounted, air-cooled Corvair engine. It obviously aimed at the success of the VW Minibus. Other cars in the picture are Corvair Lakewood and Impala Convertible.

11D: **Chrysler** New body style for the Chrysler Compact Car Valiant with 4-door Station Wagon. The 2-door Hardtop and the 2- and 4-door sedan completed the range for 1961.

11B Chevrolet Impala Sport Sedan

11D Chrysler Valiant Station Wagon

1961
page 12

12C: **Dodge** Lancer ancestry was not hard to tell. It showed Valiant body with different front grille, but without fake spare wheel in boot lid. Powered by slanted Six engine.

12D: **Dodge** Dart Pioneer, Model 6 PD 3-M, the Seneca and the Phoenix formed the Dart series. The Polara was the bigger-engined version with a very strong resemblance to the Dart.

12E: **Ford** Sunliner Convertible, based on Galaxie mechanics. Available with V-8 Thunderbird engine, up to 300 bhp.

12A Chrysler 300 G

12C Dodge Lancer

12B Desoto Two-door Hardtop

12D Dodge Dart Pioneer Station Wagon

12A: **Chrysler** 300 G, Model RC.4-P, was the successor to 300 F and based on New Yorker. Two four-barrel carbs fed the 375-bhp engine to give it a top speed of well over 150 mph. It was one of the most powerful passenger car engines on the market.

12B: **DeSoto** featured new frontal styling for 1961. Compression ratio was cut so that regular petrol could be used. Chrysler Corporation discontinued DeSoto production in December 1961.

12E Ford Sunliner

1961

13A: **Ford** Thunderbird for 1961 featured new styling and some technical improvements. From this model onwards, manual transmission was no longer available on the Thunderbird.

13B: **Imperial** Crown for 1961 featured new body styling which even in the US press was referred to as 'wild'. No new power plant for 1961.

13A Ford Thunderbird

13D Mercury Monterey

13B Imperial Crown

13E Oldsmobile F-85

13C Lincoln Continental

13C: **Lincoln** introduced a completely redesigned and very smooth-looking Continental for 1961. The car was of unit body construction and required no chassis lubrication. Even the Convertible had 4 doors, the only one of this type on the market.

13D: **Mercury** underwent a complete styling change in the preceding three or four years. Mercury Meteor 600 was sold in the low-priced field, the Meteor 800 was a little more costly, but even the top of the range Monterey, was still a medium-priced car. No chassis lubrication was needed for up to 30,000 miles.

13E: **Oldsmobile's** F-85 was very similar to Buick Special. It also featured the same all-aluminium 3·5-litre V-8 engine.

1961

14A: **Oldsmobile** Super '88' was one of 18 different models in the full-size Olds range for 1961. Body styling had been completely revised. Engine size in Rocket '88' series had been increased to 394 CID; compression ratio was down to 8.75 to 1 for operation on regular petrol.

14B: **Plymouth** Fury was one of 19 in the range and showed a very bold styling trend, emphasizing especially the front end. The tail fins had finally disappeared.

14A Oldsmobile Super '88' Holiday Sedan

14B Plymouth Fury

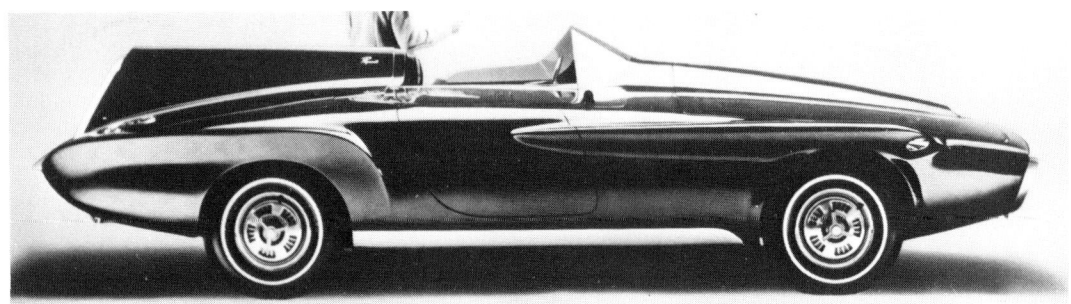

14C Plymouth XNR

14C Plymouth XNR

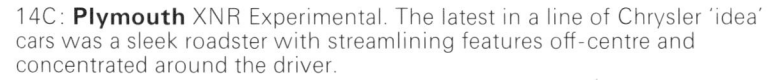

14C: **Plymouth** XNR Experimental. The latest in a line of Chrysler 'idea' cars was a sleek roadster with streamlining features off-centre and concentrated around the driver.

14D: **Pontiac** Tempest all-new compact, sharing body with Buick Special and Olds F-85. The Tempest featured a transaxle layout and offered a 195 CID 112-bhp 4-cylinder engine which had the exact bore and stroke dimensions of their own 390 CID V-8. Another very unusual feature was the use of a flexible prop. shaft.

14D Pontiac Tempest

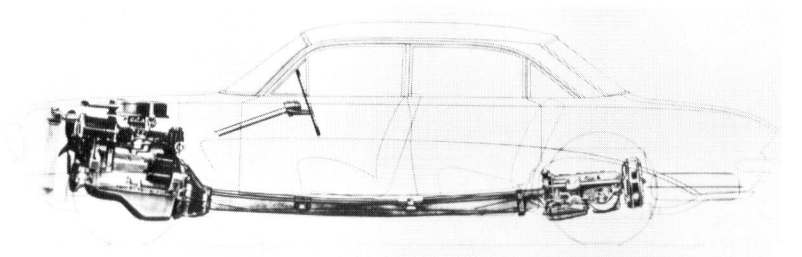

14D Pontiac Tempest

15A Pontiac Bonneville Hardtop

15B Rambler American Convertible

15C: **Rambler** Ambassador featured a restyled front end with one-piece aluminium grille, flanked by bold dual headlights. Available with a choice of two V-8 power plants of 250 and 270 bhp only; manual gearbox, overdrive, or automatic transmission options. Two different body styles: 4-door Sedan and 4-door Wagon.

15D: **Studebaker** Lark had no significant technical novelties for 1961, but a few styling improvements including an enlarged glass area. Note twin headlamps.

15A: **Pontiac** Bonneville is the top of the range model with a 123-in. wheelbase. It featured one V-8 engine of 390 CID in different versions from 215 to 348 bhp.

15B: **Rambler** American Convertible was the smallest soft-top US car on the market. It was offered with the same 195 CID six-in-line, featuring 90 and 125 bhp. Automatic transmission available. Five inches were dropped from the overall length, without loss of interior space however.

15C Rambler Ambassador V-8

15D Studebaker Lark Regal

1962

In 1962 total car sales were down again to 6,250,000, with the Chevrolet Impala as America's top-selling car. More models on one basic body were typical for 1962 production. The Big Three and AMC together offered nearly 400 models on a relatively low number of series. Chevrolet introduced its first intermediate, the Chevy II, while Ford came out with the new Fairlane 500, not exactly an intermediate, but appreciably smaller than previous Fairlanes. Chrysler gratefully used the Dart body shell as a base for a completely new body line as the previous year's models didn't sell too well.

Most other cars were changed in detail only, and Ford director Ben Mills, at the introduction of the virtually unaltered 1962 Continental explained that 'changes for the sake of changing' were just not on. They had to be 'sensible and worth while'. Despite the fact that both the Chevy II and the new Fairlane came out with full unit body construction, which AMC had had for many years, did not mean that the whole of the American car industry followed suit, if only because of the huge tooling investment that had to be made.

Much attention was given to corrosion protection on existing unit bodies. American Motors and Chrysler refined their dipping processes, while General Motors and Ford used galvanized steel in critical underbody rust areas. Particularly interesting was the development of 'sealed for life' chassis that should last 30,000 miles or three years, i.e. the average ownership of the original buyer. Oil changes every 6000 miles only were part of the new scheme. Ford had put a lot of money into the development of this, though it was admitted that time rather than mileage could kill the whole idea. As was said at the time, a chassis could easily last 100,000 miles without much attention if only the distance was covered in one year! Chrysler remained active in the development of its turbine-powered car, using a turbine-powered Dodge Dart to drive around the world for testing and publicity reasons.

16A: **Buick** Special Convertible, Model 4167, was the only 2-door soft top in the Special series consisting of five different models. It was also the latest addition to the range. Detail changes for 1962 only.

16B: **Buick** Electra 225 Riviera Sedan, Model 4829, offered three models for 1962. Turbine-Drive transmission, power steering and power brakes were standard features. Wildcat V-8 engine offered 319 bhp.

16C: **Cadillac**, Series 62 Convertible, Model 6267E, featured only minor detail changes for 1962 such as the front grille. One V-8 engine (6·4 litres) was available matching the standard Hydramatic automatic transmission. The top was power operated. Other models for 1962 were the Fleetwood Special Model 6039, Sixty Two Hardtop Sedan with 6 and with 4 windows, Models 6229 and 6239, the Sixty Two Town Sedan Model 6289 and the 75 Imperial Sedan, Model 6733.

16A Buick Special Convertible

16B Buick Electra 225

16C Cadillac Series 62 Convertible

17A: Chevrolet Chevy II was first introduced in October 1961 to bridge the increasing gap between the Corvair and the ever-growing Bel-Air and Impala series. Available with 4-cylinder 91-bhp Super Thrift and 6-cylinder 122-bhp High-Thrift engines with standard manual three-speed (or 2-speed) Powerglide. Automatic transmission optional.

17B: Chevrolet Impala, Model 1839E, featured detail changes only. Engine options varied from 170 bhp 283 CID to 409 bhp 409 CID V-8 only. Two-speed Powerglide automatic transmission was optional. It was the US car sales leader of that year.

17C: Chevrolet Corvette had a slightly modified body and was the last of the real Corvettes. One V-8 engine with four power options was available, ranging from 250 bhp to 360 bhp, the latter featuring Rochester fuel injection and a compression ratio of 11·25:1.

17C Chevrolet Corvette

17A Chevrolet Chevy II '300'

17B Chevrolet Impala Sports Sedan

17D Chrysler New Yorker

17D: Chrysler New Yorker, Model SC3-H, retained front-end styling, with canted headlights, though the fins were finally replaced by smooth rear quarters. Available with two power options: 413 CID 'Firepower' and '300 High Performance'.

1962
page 18

18A Chrysler 300 H

18C Dodge Polara 500

18A: **Chrysler** 300 H, Model SC2-M, was equipped with a ram-induction, 413 CID V-8 engine and a special heavy-duty suspension. It was the eighth in a series of Chrysler high-performance cars.

18B: **Dodge** Turbo Dart was powered by Chrysler's CR2A gas turbine engine—a development programme which, at Chrysler, started as early as 1953. In the car is George Huebner, the engineer who directed the company's gas turbine development programme.

18C: **Dodge** Polara 500 2-door Hardtop, Model PD2-H, was hard to distinguish from Dart series, with which it shared the body shell. Apart from Dart and Polara, other series were Lancer and Custom 880, with the Dart offering the more complete programme including two Wagons and a Convertible. All were available with 6 and V-8 engines, except for Custom Series which was fitted with 270-bhp 318 V-8 with four-barrel carb.

18D: **Ford** Falcon 1962 was not exported to Europe. The Futura Sports model offered standard bucket seats and 101-bhp Falcon and 170 Special Six options. Standard fitting was 85-bhp Falcon 144 Six engine with 3-speed manual transmission. Four-speed manual and 2-speed Fordomatic were optional.

18B Dodge Turbo Dart

18D Ford Falcon Futura

1962

19A Ford Fairlane 500 Town Sedan

19A: Ford Fairlane for 1962 had a much reduced wheelbase (115·5 in.) compared with the previous year when it was of the same size as Galaxie models. There were five models and three power plants, one six and two V-8's, all three performing on regular grade fuel. Manual 3-speed was standard with all models; overdrive with automatic 4th gear and 2-speed Fordomatic were optional.

19B: Ford Galaxie offered a choice of three Wagons for 1962 with either six- or nine-seater capacity. Ranch Wagon seating six only, Country Sedan and Country Squire—the latter distinguished by walnut-grained steel panels on body sides and available with optional Thunderbird 390 Special V-8 engine and Cruise-O-Matic Drive.

19B Ford Galaxie Country Sedan

19C Imperial Le Baron

19C: Imperial Le Baron featured detail changes only to chassis and body for 1962. For this year the tail fins had completely disappeared, the new rear-quarter panels showing dart-like tail lights. The power plant was the same as in the Chrysler New Yorker, 350-bhp V-8. Other models were Imperial Custom and Imperial Crown.

19D: Lincoln for 1962 had the same chassis and uncluttered lines as in 1961. The Continental was the only 4-door convertible on the market. It was of unit body construction. The power plant was a 7-litre V-8 offering a smooth 304 bhp.

19D Lincoln Continental Convertible

1962

20A: Mercury Comet series, virtually unchanged, offered 2- and 4-door Sedans and 2- and 4-door Wagons. Choice of 2 engines: Standard '6' (86 bhp) and optional '170 6' (102 bhp). Standard 3-speed manual or optional Merc-O-Matic drive automatic transmission.

20B: Mercury offered three main series: compact Comet, medium-size Meteor and regular Monterey. Three main body styles and four engines (6 and V-8) were offered on Monterey. Two service intervals: 6000 miles for oil change and 30,000 miles, or twice a year, were introduced.

20A Mercury Comet

20C: Oldsmobile F-85, Model 3167, as a Cutlass convertible, was available in three more models: Sedan, Coupé and Station Wagon. Of the aluminium 3·5-litre V-8 engine, two versions were offered: standard 155 bhp and high compression (10·25:1) 188 bhp with four-barrel downdraft carb.

20D: Oldsmobile '98' was one of the three regular Oldsmobile series which also offered a Super '88', Dynamic '88' and top of the range Starfire. Based on the Bel-Air/Impala body shell, all three series comprised sixteen models powered by the V-8 'Skyrocket' engine in three power versions from 260 bhp to 335 bhp. Four-speed Hydramatic automatic transmission standard on Super '88', '98' and Starfire models.

20B Mercury Monterey Custom

20C Oldsmobile F-85 Cutlass

20D Oldsmobile '98' Holiday Sports Sedan

1962

21A: **Plymouth** Valiant, Model SV1-H, was originally introduced as Chrysler Valiant in 1960 and was moved over—marketing wise—to the Plymouth division in 1961, being marketed as Valiant that year. With detail changes only, it showed the Valiant badge on the front grille and Plymouth on the new rear deck lid. Only one (6-cylinder) engine was offered with two transmission options: manual and automatic.

21B: **Plymouth** Savoy, Belvedere and Fury dropped their unsuccessful 1961 body shell completely for model year 1962 in favour of the more compact Dart series body from Dodge. They differed only in styling details such as the front grille. Shown is the Sport Fury Hardtop, Model B 582-H.

21C: **Plymouth** top-range Fury featured five body styles including two Station Wagons: a 6- and a 9-seater. V-8 power plants for Fury were Fury V-800, Super Fury V-800 and Golden Commando. Front suspension was on torsion bars; rear suspension consisted of live axle on leaf springs. Shown here is Fury Suburban, Model SP2 H-45.

21A Plymouth Valiant 200

21D: **Pontiac** Tempest, Model 2119, changed in detail only. The 3·2-litre OHV 4-cylinder engine was offered with a choice of three transmissions: standard manual 3-speed, with synchromesh on 2nd and 3rd, optional fully synchronized 4-speed manual and optional Tempestorque automatic transmission. The full Tempest range consisted of four models: Sedan and Station Wagon, Le Mans Coupé and Convertible. Tempest was the only compact that was left with a 4-cylinder engine availability.

21B Plymouth Sport Fury Hardtop

21C Plymouth Fury Suburban Station Wagon

21D Pontiac Tempest

1962

page 22

22A Pontiac Catalina Vista

22A: **Pontiac** regular models changed front- and rear-end styling for 1962. Shown here is Catalina Vista Model 2339. Other regular models for 1962 were Strato Six-powered Laurentian and Parisienne (Canadian) series and V-8 powered (choice of seven), Bonneville, Star Chief, Catalina and Grand Prix, the latter being completely new for 1962. This totalled seventeen models for the North American market.

22B Rambler American 400

22C Rambler Renault

22D Studebaker Avanti

22B: **Rambler** American 400 was offered in six versions with one 195·6 CID 6-cylinder engine. Shown here is the 400 4-door Sedan.
22C: **Rambler** Renault was a shrewd but not successful attack by American Motors Corporation to sell US cars on the European market through the French Renault organisation. The car, derived from the 1962 Rambler Classic Custom Sedan, crossed the ocean in CKD form and was assembled in a Belgian Renault assembly plant. It was originally offered with a 3·2-litre 6-cylinder engine and a manual 3-speed gearbox.
22D: **Studebaker** Avanti was the latest styling exercise by the famous Raymond Loewy on a modified Lark Daytona chassis. The reinforced fibre-glass body made the car light and strong. It was the first US production car to provide caliper disc brakes as standard equipment. The Avanti featured 289 CID 280-bhp V-8 with manual 3-speed or optional manual 4-speed or 3-speed automatic transmission. Next to the car are designer Raymond Loewy (left) and Sherwood Egbert, president of Studebaker Corporation and a major force behind the Avanti project.

1963

Sales were up again in 1963, totalling 7,644,403 units, with Chevrolet's Impala still being the top-selling car. There were few completely new bodies (mostly refinements), but a notable addition of sports models such as the **Buick Riviera** and the **Studebaker Avanti** which in fact had already been introduced in 1962. Chevrolet provided small quantities of its regular models with an aluminium radiator block and completely restyled the Corvette into the striking new Stingray. Mercury Monterey adopted a new body and, apart from a new concave grille, it sported a remarkable rear window style with reverse slant and overhang.

Much work had been done on better quality in connection with rust-proofing and body rattles, etc. More corrosion-resistant materials were used and rubber bushes added to suspension and chassis.

Engineering advancement, more than anything else, was put into better performance and economy, longer-lasting materials, stronger and quieter engines and the adoption of alternators as standard or optional equipment and in one case—the Avanti—even disc brakes. Amber turn indicators replaced the old, clear ones as they were much easier to see both by day and by night. The word safety belt was also mentioned again, although not too strongly.

23B Buick Riviera

transmission. Series 62, 63 and 75 offered Convertible, Sedan de Ville, Coupé de Ville and Imperial Limousine body styles respectively.
23D: Cadillac Sedan de Ville, Series 63, Model 6329 with a different roof line treatment.

23A Buick Special    23C Cadillac Special Fleetwood

23A: Buick Special, Model 449, showed 3·9 in. longer body on the same wheelbase as the previous year. Body styling too was changed, showing fewer curves. Engine choice was between 3·2-litre V-6 and 3·5-litre aluminium V-8.
23B: Buick Riviera, Model 4747E, was an exciting new Coupé body with a strong Italian styling influence. It offered 4 bucket seats, automatic transmission and a 6·5-litre V-8 developing 330 bhp.
23C: Cadillac Special Fleetwood Series 60, Model 6039, continued the previous year's body styling. Note however the flattened windscreen. The side tail fins have disappeared. Cadillac offered one 6·4-litre V-8 engine coupled to a 4-speed Hydramatic automatic

23D Cadillac Sedan de Ville

1963

24A: Checker is a typical taxicab manufacturer who does not exactly follow contemporary fashion. Based on their latest (1958) body shell, the company developed an enormous 6- or 8-door Aerobus for 9- or 12-passenger transport to and from airports. It was powered by a 6-cylinder Continental side valve engine; the longest version had a wheelbase of 188 in. and was 265 in. long.

24A Checker 9-passenger Aerobus

24B Chevrolet Corvair Testudo

24B: Chevrolet Corvair drew the attention of several Italian body specialists. This one is a styling exercise by Nuccio Bertone, and was named the 'Testudo'.
24C: Chevrolet Corvair in yet another guise; the famous Italian stylist Pinin Farina designed this smooth body on the Corvair Monza.

24C Chevrolet Corvair

24D Chevrolet, Chevy II, Nova 400

24D: Chevrolet Chevy II, Model 449, with only minor detail changes for 1963. It was offered with 4- and 6-cylinder engines. Built of unit body construction and with live rear axle.

25A Chevrolet range

25C Chrysler New Yorker

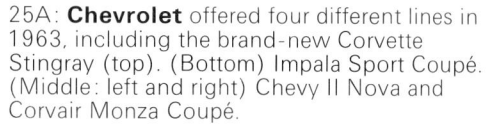

25A: **Chevrolet** offered four different lines in 1963, including the brand-new Corvette Stingray (top). (Bottom) Impala Sport Coupé. (Middle: left and right) Chevy II Nova and Corvair Monza Coupé.

25B: **Chevrolet** Corvette offered a completely new fibre-glass body styling on new Stingray, which still had its separate chassis, but with IRS for the first time.

25C: **Chrysler** New Yorker, Model TL3-H, featured a completely new body styling. Gone were the canted headlights, though the square front remained. Other regulars were Newport and 300 series, powered by V-8 engines only.

25D: **Chrysler** was very serious with its turbine engine project. This latest version was given on loan in small numbers to a carefully selected group of drivers for normal driving test purposes, in order to draw the opinion from the man in the street.

25B Chevrolet Corvette Stingray

25D Chrysler Turbine

1963 page 26

26A Dodge Dart GT

26C Dodge Polara 4-door Hardtop

26A: **Dodge** Dart GT, Model TL1-P, replaced the Lancer series. Technically similar to the Valiant series, Dart GT was a stronger and faster version, and available with 6-cylinder 145-bhp Power-Pack engine. Also available as GT Convertible.

26B: **Dodge** 330 was available with either six-in-line or V-8 engine. Wheelbase and body dimensions were the same as those of the Polara series.

26C: **Dodge** Polara, Model TD2-P, had same 119-in. wheelbase as other cars in 1963 Dodge range. Biggest Dodge models of the year were 880 Custom Series featuring V-8 265 bhp, and Special High Performance V-8 power plants, ranging up to 425 bhp, a compression ratio of 14·5:1 and two four-barrel carbs.

26D: **Ford** Falcon Futura Sedan was a new addition to 1963 Falcon range. The new Thunderbird roof line was used on all Falcon Sedans for 1963. The range also included for the first time a Convertible and a Squire (Station Wagon) version and was available with 2·4-litre 6-cylinder engines from 85 bhp onwards.

26B Dodge 330

26D Ford Falcon Futura Sedan

27A Ford Falcon 'Clan'

27A: **Ford** Falcon 'Clan' by Pinin Farina clearly showed keen interest in US-built cars by Italian body stylists. This car was displayed at the 1963 Turin Motor Show.
27B: **Ford** Fairlane 500 Sports Coupé had been added to the Fairlane series, together with three new wagons. Note the Thunderbird styled roof line. The need for a 1000-mile inspection had been eliminated, while major chassis lubrication intervals had been increased to 36,000 miles, with minor lubrication and oil changes at 6000 miles. Engine options ranged from the standard 101-bhp 6-cylinder to 164-bhp V-8.

27C Ford Galaxie 500 4-door Hardtop

27C: **Ford** Galaxie range comprised 8 models, a choice of 6 engines and 5 transmissions, including America's first fully synchronized manual 3-speed. Also Galaxie featured Ford's twice-a-year or 6000-mile service schedule. There was one 223 CID 6 of 138 bhp; the V-8 power plants ranged from 260 CID 164 bhp to 406 CID with 405 bhp, the C.R. of the latter (a hotted-up Thunderbird version) being 11·5:1.
27D: **Ford** Mustang prototype with 100-bhp Ford Taunus V-4 engine. It was publicly launched in Europe at the 1963 Geneva Motor Show, but never reached the production stage. The final Mustang did not appear until almost a year later and bore very little resemblance to this car. Inside the car is H. L. Misch, leader of construction team. Next to the car is Gene Bordinat, head of the styling department.

27B Ford Fairlane 500 Sports Coupé

27D Ford Mustang Experimental

1963
page 28

28A: Imperial Le Baron 4-door Hardtop, Model TY1-H, was hardly changed for 1963. Note panoramic windshield and restyled roof, to allow higher rear seats and greater rear headroom.

28B: Jeep Wagoneer by Willys Motors Inc. which was an all-new Jeep Station Wagon Series intended for passenger transportation. It offered an automatic transmission with 4-wheel drive—a unique combination in automotive history. Two-wheel drive was also available, with automatic transmission as an optional extra, plus a 2-door body style.

28C: Lincoln Continental added detail refinements to their 1963 range, but did little to change outer appearance, apart from front grille. Shown here is a formal Executive Limousine with special long wheelbase.

28D: Mercury completely restyled the Monterey for 1963. It featured a unique rear window and roof line, the window slanting inward and power-operated, providing additional ventilation when opened. Rear overhang also cured rain and snow visibility problems.

28E: Oldsmobile 98 Series, Model 3847E, was Oldsmobile's top of the range. Other regulars were Super 88 and Starfire. A completely new body with uncluttered lines, this Olds was one of the first of a new design period.

28A Imperial Le Baron

28B Jeep Wagoneer

28C Lincoln Continental Executive Limousine

28D Mercury Monterey

28E Oldsmobile 98 Holiday Sport Coupé

1963

29A: **Plymouth** Valiant, Model TV1-H, showed a fresh new body style. V-100, V-200 and Signet 200 were powered by a 101-bhp six-in-line engine. Special 145-bhp Power Pack was available on Economy Six. New in the range was a Signet 200 Convertible.

29B: **Pontiac** Tempest, Model 2119, had clean, square line of enlarged body on same wheelbase. Standard 4-cylinder, but now also with optional V-8 for Tempest Le Mans.

29C: **Pontiac** Grand Prix was built on Catalina chassis. Choice of various V-8 engine options. New for 1963: modified rear suspension with coil springs. V-8 6·9-litre 375-bhp engine available, with three downdraught twin carbs. Also available with Hurst 'dual-gate' control for manual and automatic transmission.

29D: **Rambler** Classic Six offered new, modern and low body on 550, 660 and 770 series, featuring a longer wheelbase with the same body length. In Europe also available as Rambler Renault.

29E: **Studebaker** Hawk was offered with an option of 6- and V-8 engines. New radiator grille for 1963, grille panels and ornaments. Caliper disc brakes were optional on the Hawk, as they were on all 1963 Studebaker cars, with the exception of the Avanti, which had these as a standard fitting.

29A Plymouth Valiant V-200

29B Pontiac Tempest

29C Pontiac Grand Prix

29D Rambler Classic 770 Sedan

29E Studebaker Hawk Gran Turismo

1964 Car sales were slightly down again, only just reaching the 7 million mark. Apart from one or two cars such as the Corvair and the Rambler American (though even the latter had grown a little) it seemed that compacts were no longer in business in 1964. Now being called 'senior compacts', Dodge had increased the Dart to intermediate size as had Buick's Special, Oldsmobile's F-85 and Pontiac's Tempest, following the trend of growth. Even that lovely 4-cylinder Tempest power plant was no longer available in 1964.

Several new engines were introduced but the use of aluminium was down the line a bit with both Chrysler and GM dropping some aluminium blocks in favour of cast-iron. Manual transmissions were still available, even in combination with some of the biggest V-8's, while Plymouth were now even building their own manual transmission.

Dodge celebrated their golden anniversary, whereas Studebaker, facing severe troubles, closed their factories in South Bend and moved over to Hamilton in Canada where 17,614 cars were built. Power units now came from GM. (Including the Avanti Jet Thrust. See page 37.)

Three completely new cars were introduced in 1964 and various others such as the AMC American underwent an extensive reshape. Chevrolet launched the Chevelle series, Chrysler announced the Plymouth Barracuda in May, while Ford had already introduced their Mustang to the public one month earlier. It wasn't exactly the car that everyone was expecting, although good looking. Again these cars showed that many Americans still liked to get some fun out of driving.

30A Buick Special

30B Buick Electra 225

30C Cadillac Fleetwood Eldorado Convertible

30D Cadillac Sedan de Ville

30A: **Buick** Special, Model 4169, wheelbase 3 in. longer and almost 12 in. more overall.
30B: **Buick** Electra 7, Model 4847 CM, longer, lower and wider for 1964. The grille and rear fenders had been restyled and the new Turbine 400 torque converter transmission was standard equipment on all Electra models and Riviera.
30C: **Cadillac** Fleetwood Eldorado Convertible, Model 6267, adopted a sporty look. Engine capacity was increased to 7 litres, power output to 345 bhp. The new Turbo-Hydramatic transmission was standard on series 60, 63 and 62 Hydramatic.
30D: **Cadillac** Series 62, detail improvements included rear-axle location.

1964

31A: **Checker** came in two series: A12 and A12W, with 6- or 8-passenger capacity. Choice of new OHV 6-cylinder or V-8 4·6-litre engine from Chevrolet. Standard with manual 3-speed (synchromesh on 2nd and 3rd), or 3-speed Single Range automatic transmission. LWB version A-12E and Aerobus A-12W6C and A-12W8L (6 or 8 doors) completed the Checker range.

31B: **Chevrolet** Corvair Monza Spyder, Model 627AT, was one of 7 Corvair models plus 2 Greenbriers Sports Wagons. New grille and front-end ornamentation distinguished the 1964 series.

31C: **Chevrolet** Chevelle Malibu Sedan, Model 5569 Ck, was one of Chevrolet's latest range, which made five separate and distinct lines for this top-selling GM division. It was the only all-new car to arrive on the scene for 1964. Built on a 115-in. wb and coming in three series: Chevelle 300, Malibu and Malibu SS, with 11 different models, two 6-cylinder engines and two versions of the 283 CID V-8 engine. Four transmission options were offered.

31A Checker Marathon Sedan

31B Chevrolet Corvair Monza Spyder

31C Chevrolet Chevelle Malibu

31D Chrysler New-Yorker

31D: **Chrysler** New-Yorker, Model VC3-H, with different front- and rear-end treatment, but similar razor lines giving a much cleaner effect. Detail modifications on chassis. Same wheelbase but slightly shorter body.

1964

page 32

32A Dodge Polara 500 Hardtop

32B Dodge Custom 880 Convertible

32C Ford Falcon Sprint

32D Ford Fairlane 500 Sedan

32A: **Dodge** Polara, Model VD1-H. New hardtop roof line, different grille and rear-end treatment were the new major changes. Rear track had been widened by 2·1 in.

32B: **Dodge** Custom 880, Model VA3-L.27, had lower and longer profile, while overall length had been increased by 1·7 in. Series 880 comprised 4-door Sedan VA3-E41, 5-door Station Wagon 6-seat A3-E45, 5-door Station Wagon VA; Series Custom 880: 2-door Hardtop (Faux Cabriolet) VA3-L-23, 2-door Convertible Coupé VA3-L-27, 4-door Sedan VA3-L-41, 4-door Faux Cabriolet, VA3-L-43, Hardtop Station Wagon, 6-seats, VA3-L-45, Hardtop Station Wagon, 9-seats, VA3-L-46. There was a choice of two V-8 engines and three transmissions.

32C: **Ford** Falcon Sprint, restyled for 1964, offered 17 models in 5 series including 2- and 4-door Sedans, Hardtops, Sports Coupés, Convertibles, Station Wagons, Station Bus, Club Wagon and De Luxe Club Wagon. They featured a 260 CID V-8 engine as standard equipment.

32D: **Ford** Fairlane 500 Sedan, Model 62 B, had improved engine performance and featured styling changes for 1964. Five engines available, including two 289 CID V-8, plus 170 and 220 CID 6-cylinder engines. Also five transmissions were offered as well as eight body styles.

1964

33A Ford Galaxie 500/XL 4-door Hardtop

33B Ford Mustang II

33C Imperial Crown Hardtop

33D Mercury Comet Caliente Hardtop

33A: **Ford** Galaxie 500/XL 4-door Hardtop, Model 57C, was, including Custom, Custom 500, Galaxie 500 and Station Wagon, one of sixteen body options on the same basic body shell. A range of engines was offered from the 223 CID 6-cylinder to the 427 CID high performance V-8
33B: **Ford** Mustang arrived in April 1964 and sold for under $3000. Its wheelbase was 108 in. and overall length 181·6 in. There were two models: Convertible and Hardtop, and four power plants from which to choose: standard 170 CID 6-cylinder and three V-8's: 260 CID 160 bhp, 289 CID 240 bhp and 289 CID 271 bhp, the latter being a Cobra-developed engine with special power to weight ratio.
33C: **Imperial** Crown Hardtop, Model VY-M-43, was completely restyled for 1964. With Crown and Le Baron there were 4 models: Crown VY 1-M-23 2-door Hardtop, VY 1-M-27 2-door Convertible, VY 1-M-43 4-door Hardtop and Le Baron VY 1-H-43 4-door Hardtop. Convertible model was a new addition for 1964.
33D: **Mercury** Comet Caliente Hardtop, Model 63 C, was one of three models. A new 3-speed automatic transmission and four engines including two new ones: 289 CID V-8 and 200 CID six were available. The 1964 Comet offered 10 models in three new series designations: Comet 202, Comet 404 and Comet Caliente, as top of the line.

1964

34A: Mercury offered six V-8 engines, two more than in 1963, ranging from 250 to 425 bhp. Other ranges apart from Montclair were Comet, Monterey, Parklane, Commuter and Colony Park. Experimental car was Super Marauder. Complete Mercury programme comprised 44 models.

34B Oldsmobile F-85 Vista Cruiser Station Wagon

34B: Oldsmobile F-85 series, Model 3055, sported the new Vista Cruiser Station Wagon with either 6 or 8 seats. Standard engine size, Jet-fire Rocket 230 bhp V-8, and an option of 290 bhp. Three transmissions were available. Oldsmobile also offered a new economic V-6 engine.

34C: Oldsmobile Dynamic 88 Holiday Sedan, Model 3469, shared its body shell with the Jetstar 88, but featured a bigger V-8 of 6·5-litre capacity. A manual 3-speed transmission was still a standard fitting. Other Oldsmobile full-size series were: Jetstar 88, Super 88, Jetstar I, Starfire and Series 98.

34D: Plymouth Valiant V-200 Sedan, Model VVI-H-41, featured detail changes only. It was technically close to Dodge Dart models and for the first time it was available with a 4·5-litre V-8 engine, with an optional manual 4-speed transmission. Standard engine was 2·8-litre 101 bhp six-in-line.

34A Mercury Montclair Hardtop

34C Oldsmobile Dynamic 88

34D Plymouth Valiant V-200

35A Plymouth Barracuda

35B Plymouth Sport Fury two-door Hardtop.

35A: Plymouth Barracuda was a new Sports Coupé based on the Valiant body shell and mechanics, with a new type of fast back styling. It was introduced in May 1964 and could be regarded as a direct answer to Ford's Mustang. Engine and transmission options were the same as for Valiant apart from special Hurst competition linkage. Basic price remained under $2500!

35B: Plymouth Sport Fury Hardtop, Model VP-H-23, was one of six models of the same series. Savoy, Belvedere, Fury and Sport Fury were the V-8 cars and only minor details were changed for 1964. Rear track had been widened by 2·1 in.

35D Pontiac Star Chief

35C: Pontiac Tempest Custom, Model 2169, grew considerably for 1964 as did its Buick and Oldsmobile counterparts. The compact idea seemed long forgotten. Also the 4-cylinder engine was no longer available.

35D: Pontiac Star Chief 4-door Hardtop, Model 2639, was also available as a 4-door Sedan. There was a choice of nine V8 engines as well as a selection of 3- and 4-speed manual transmissions and one automatic (Hydramatic 315) transmission.

35C Pontiac Tempest Custom Four-door Sedan

1964

36A: **Pontiac** Grand Prix was top of the line model and was offered with manual 3- and 4-speed transmissions on 306-bhp V-8 engine, with Hydramatic 375 only coupled to the 230-bhp version, whereas all three transmission variants could be delivered with further engine options: 303 bhp, 350 bhp, 320 bhp and 370 bhp.

36B: **Rambler** American 440 and 440 H series were completely new for 1964. A 138-bhp 6-cylinder engine was standard on 440-H models and optional on all other 'Americans'. In addition to the Hardtop illustrated, 'Americans' were offered in five Sedan models, two Station Wagons and one Convertible.

36C: **Rambler** Classic 770 4-door with front- and rear-end modifications and other body detail changes. The Hardtop was new for 1964 and an optional aluminium engine was available. It was offered with 127- and 138-bhp 6-cylinder engines, normally with a choice of manual, semi-automatic or Flash-O-Matic automatic transmission. Classic Six Series were 550, 660 and 770, with twelve variations.

36D: **Rambler** Ambassador 990 4-door Station Wagon with a V-8 250 bhp engine as standard and a 270 bhp version as an option. A full range of transmissions was available, including the new Shift Command unit which could be shifted manually or set as a fully automatic unit.

36A Pontiac Grand Prix Sports Coupé

36B Rambler American

36C Rambler Classic 770

36D Rambler Ambassador Station Wagon

37A: Studebaker Challenger and Commander 6 and V-8, Commander Model 64S-F4 shown, were basic Studebaker series. There was a choice of one 6 and six V-8 engines, among which were a blown version and the 5-litre Avanti 'Jet Thrust R 3 and 4'. South Bend factory was closed and Studebaker moved to Hamilton, Canada, where 17,614 units were built in 1964.

37B: Studebaker Cruiser was the top of the range series and was built on the longer Station Wagon chassis. It was offered with a choice of V-8's only up to 5-litre Avanti engines, 'Jet Thrust R 3 and 4'. Only one 4-door Sedan (longer wheelbase) body was available.

37C: Studebaker Hawk, with yet again a number of detail changes to front- and rear-end, plus a new vinyl roof to distinguish this from the previous year's model. Engine options were the same as for Cruiser, excluding 'Jet Thrust 4'. Four types of transmission were offered including an overdrive and the Flight-O-Matic 3-speed automatic transmission.

37A Studebaker Commander

37B Studebaker Cruiser

37C Studebaker Gran Turismo Hawk

1965

Together with truck sales, US motor vehicle sales as a whole exceeded the 10 million mark in one year for the first time! The trend for 1965 was: more variety, more power and yet again a few added inches.

Ralph Nader, the lawyer whose name and action was feared throughout the entire US car industry as well as by some major importers, raised his voice once again. His book *Unsafe at any speed*, derived from a consumer's report of a somewhat earlier date, prompted Congress to rethink about the powerful car industry. Into every car price went at least a sum of $125 per car, representing the cost for annual changes. The public was willing to pay because it was willing to change, as Elwood Engel, chief stylist of the Chrysler Corporation put it, explaining that this was what made America a great country. If every American was willing to drive an identical, comfortable compact car he could probably have this car for less than $1000. But so long as the average customer enters the showroom with the intention of buying a standard compact, and then as a reward for his frugality dresses it up with an air-conditioner, power brakes, power steering, automatic transmission and an optional V-8, it is a mobile status symbol to him and not just 'wheels'.

Technical sophistication was another important trend in 1965. Power brakes and power steering were more in demand and even the disc brake was catching up in popularity. Though the customer spent a lot of money on tinted windows, air-conditioners and many other optional extras to dress up his car, the industry had already started to invest huge sums in safety.

38A: **Buick** Wildcat Hardtop Coupé sold on the sporty side of the immense Buick range. On a lengthened wheelbase it was one of seven models, namely three Sedans, one Hardtop Sedan, two Hardtop Coupés and one Convertible. It came with a 375-bhp 6·5-litre V-8 engine as standard and a choice of three transmissions. The automatic version was the Super Turbine '400'.

38B: **Buick** Riviera appeared to have given its styling to all GM Divisions for 1965. The roof line was to be seen in other Buicks, also in Chevys, Pontiacs and Oldsmobiles. For 1965, Riviera concealed its headlamps behind retractable doors and the engine capacity and

38A Buick Wildcat Hardtop Coupé

power output were slightly reduced. There was, however, still a massive 325 bhp from a 6·6-litre V-8 engine. Automatic transmission only.

38C: **Cadillac** Fleetwood, Model 68069 EG, featured a new perimeter frame for 1965, with a lower centre of gravity and greater torsional rigidity. It also included a new self-levelling suspension, but Cadillac remained faithful to the live rear axle on coil springs. The Turbo-Hydramatic was now a standard fitting on all Cadillacs, and the cars offered the industry's only triple braking system.

38D: **Cadillac** de Ville, Model 68339 EG Convertible, was one of three open-air models within the Cadillac range. It used the same mechanical parts as the rest of the range.

38B Buick Riviera

38C Cadillac Fleetwood Sixty Special Sedan

38D Cadillac de Ville Convertible

39A Chevrolet Corvair Monza Convertible and Coupé Hardtop

39B Chevrolet Chevy II Nova SS Sport Coupé

39C Chevrolet Impala Station Wagon

39D Chevrolet Concours

39A: Chevrolet Corvair Monza, Model 10539 AT, featured the first major styling change since it was introduced in 1960. All types were now designated Monza, apart from the Series 500, and even the Sedan came without a centre pillar. New for 1965 was the Corsa sports model with the choice of a 180-bhp with, or 140-bhp without turbo-charger. There were seven models for 1965.

39B: Chevrolet Chevy II featured only a few styling changes. New engine options were added among which, for the first time were three V-8s. The old 90-bhp 4-cylinder remained on the list however. A new SS series was added to the line.

39C: Chevrolet Impala plus all other large Chevy models accounted for well over 33% of GM's total sales in 1964, 60% of which was Impala! Impala featured an improved body line with a faint Corvair and Corvette family resemblance. A new chassis was also used, departing from the old X-frame, which resulted in a stronger and more rigid undergear, enabling a lower body line to be used without any loss of floor space. Shown here is the Impala Station Wagon.

39D: Chevrolet Concours was a styling design based on Impala mechanics. It never went into production however.

1965

40A: Chrysler New Yorker was the oldest Chrysler series still in use. Apart from a longer wheelbase, it featured a redesigned body, a new roof line, and new front and rear treatment. The four round headlamps were neatly grouped behind etched glass windows. There were 5 New Yorkers in the range with a choice of two V-8 engines and one automatic transmission (Torque-Flite).

40B: Cord 8/10 project meant the revival of an old, famous name. From the front-wheel driving Corvair engine to the smallest mechanical detail, every part was derived from current US cars. The body was made of Expanded Royalite by the US Rubber Company and it strongly resembled the 1935–37 Cord 8/10. A small-scale series production was intended.

40C Dodge Coronet

40A Chrysler New Yorker Hardtop

40D Dodge Custom 880

40B Cord Sportsman 8/10

40C: Dodge Coronet was a new model in the range, replacing the Six. It had slightly reduced outer dimensions and obviously formed Dodge's middle-line. There were the Coronet Six, Coronet 440, Coronet V-8 and Coronet 500 Series, available in 16 models, with one 6 and six V-8s. Available transmissions were the 3-speed manual and Torque-Flite automatic transmission, with the option of a 4-speed manual, in conjunction with the 265-bhp, 330-bhp and 425-bhp power plants.

40D: Dodge Custom 880 shared the Chrysler Newport roof line. It came in five body styles, which included a Sedan, Hardtop, Convertible and Station Wagon. A new 270-bhp V-8 engine was a standard fitting, and three other options were available. In the same range were Polara and the new model, Monaco.

41A: Excalibur SS and SSK were replicas of the famous 1927–30 Mercedes Sports Car, as seen through American eyes. Designed by Brooks Stevens on a Studebaker Daytona chassis and powered by a 300-bhp Chevrolet Corvette V-8 engine, it was available with a 4-speed manual or a 3-speed Powerglide automatic transmission.

41A Excalibur SS

41B Ford Fairlane 500

41C Ford Galaxie 500 XL Convertible

41D Ford Mustang Fastback 2+2

41B: **Ford** Fairlane 500 4-door Sedan with a restyled front- and rear-end, offered two main series and eight models. Engine options ranged from a 6-cylinder 3·3-litre 120 hp unit to a 4·7-litre 271 hp V-8 with a CR of 10·9:1. Three transmission types were available on all except the two smaller models.
41C: **Ford** Galaxie featured a new perimeter frame with coil springs front and rear, and an updated body line. The Galaxie range comprised six main series, amounting to seventeen different models. One 6 and six V-8s were available, offering up to 431 bhp, the one illustrated having a CR of 14:1.
41D/E: **Ford** Mustang proved an instant success. A fastback version was new for 1965. Bertone, the Italian stylist, tried again, this time on the Mustang.

41E Ford Mustang 2+2 by Bertone

1965

page 42

42A: **Ford** Thunderbird Convertible with detail changes to body only. For 1965 the Thunderbird was the first Ford to be fitted with disc brakes as standard.

42A Ford Thunderbird Convertible

42C Lincoln Continental

42B Imperial Crown Coupé

42B: **Imperial** Crown was top of the range of all Chrysler Corporation makes, which amounted to 60 models in 1965. Note 'Lincoln-type' overhang of front fender!

42C: **Lincoln** Continental was the second Ford car featuring front disc brakes as a standard fitting. It had a redesigned front grille and front turn indicators incorporated in the fenders.

42D: **Mercury** Montclair featured a new suspension system with coil springs front and rear. The chassis was 3 in. longer. The slanting rear window was typical for the Montclair series.

42D Mercury Montclair

43A: **Mercury** was experimenting with a new steering-column—twisting instead of turning. The idea was to produce more space and less fatigue for the driver.

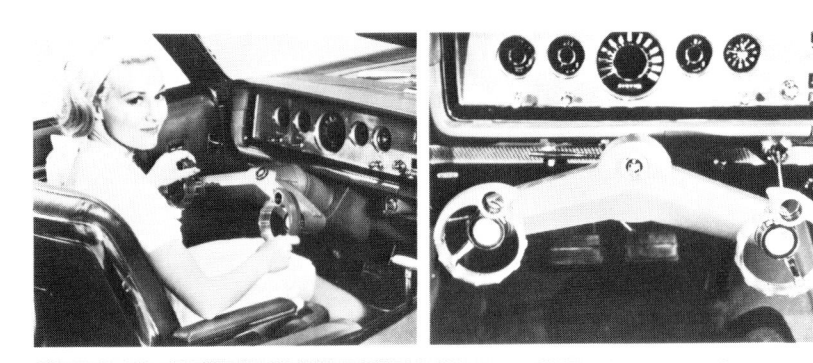

43A Mercury Park Lane Experimental

43B Oldsmobile Jetstar 88 Holiday Sedan

43C Oldsmobile Dynamic 88 Holiday Coupé

43B: **Oldsmobile** offered two sports models for 1965: the Jetstar 88 and the Dynamic 88, featuring a new powerful 7-litre engine and redesigned chassis, available with a 3- or 4-speed manual or Turbo-Hydramatic transmission. There were four Jetstar 88 body styles.

43C: **Oldsmobile** Dynamic 88 featured a redesigned chassis and a 425 CID Super Rocket engine producing 310 bhp. The roof line and rear fenders were not unlike the Riviera styling. Other series were F85 V-6 and V-8, Custom V-8, Vista Cruiser V-8, Delta 88, Jetstar 88, Jetstar I, Starfire and '98' Series. Oldsmobile offered 34 models for 1965.

43D: **Plymouth** Valiant Signet 200 Model AV1-H was one of four series, (including Barracuda) totalling ten different models. There were detail changes to the body only. Choice of two Sixes and two Eights; front disc brakes were an optional extra.

43D Plymouth Valiant Signet 200

1965
page 44

44A Plymouth Barracuda

44B Pontiac Tempest GTO

44D: **Rambler** American, having had a complete restyle in the previous year showed some minor detail changes only for 1965. There were four series: 220, 330, 440, 440H, with four 6-cylinder engines and ten models available. Shown here is the 440 4-door Sedan.

44C Pontiac Bonneville 4-door Hardtop

44A: **Plymouth** Barracuda was basically a Valiant and shared its mechanical components.
44B: **Pontiac** Tempest Le Mans GTO was a new sporty Tempest model, available with a very powerful 6·4-litre V-8 engine. There was a choice of two engines and four transmissions. Stacked headlamps was the most notable model change for 1965.
44C: **Pontiac** Bonneville 4-door Hardtop was one of the first to illustrate the famous Coke-bottle line. It had the same mechanics as the Star Chief; for 1965 it also had a longer chassis and stacked headlamps.

44D Rambler American

45A: Rambler Ambassador came in three series: 880, 990 and 990H. Available with one Six and two V-8s, there were seven models, including one Convertible as shown. The wheelbase was 4 in. longer than the Classic series. The Classic and Ambassador were easily distinguishable by stacked headlamps on the latter.

45B: Rambler Marlin was AMC's answer to the Mustang, Barracuda, etc. AMC decided that distinctive styling rather than brute power and performance would be the main feature. Front-end styling was 'Classic' and it came with the standard 232 CID 155-bhp Six. Front disc brakes were standard.

45C: Studebaker concentrated on fewer models for 1965, continuing production in Hamilton, Canada. The Hawk and Avanti series were discontinued. Two engines, supplied by GM, were offered in three series, and there were three body styles. A 120-bhp OHV Six and a 195-bhp V-8 Commander, Daytona and Cruiser Series.

45A Rambler Ambassador 990 Convertible

45B Rambler Marlin

45C Studebaker Daytona Four-door Sedan

1966

Car sales in the US were down to 9,028,000. Partly responsible for this fairly sharp decline was the fact that Studebaker's car production ceased even in its Canadian Hamilton factory. Avanti however resumed production as a separate manufacturer in South Bend, Indiana.

Dodge introduced the Charger and in fact, yet again the main theme of the US car producers was 'Bigger and Faster'. Interesting was a special Sprint version of the Pontiac Tempest, featuring an OHC in-line 6 while the long awaited disc brake became standard equipment in a few more popular models in the course of 1966.

A complete breakthrough in US car development was the exciting new front-wheel driven Toronado by Oldsmobile. Surprisingly neutral was the handling of this big car. More of the previous years' optional extras such as power steering, power brakes, air-conditioning etcetera became standard items on 'top-of-the-range' series. Oldsmobile's V-6 engine was quietly discontinued and replaced by an in-line 6. The concealed headlights gimmick which was started by Buick's Riviera was also adopted by Charger and Toronado.

46A Ambassador 990 4-door Sedan

46B AMC AMX II

46C Avanti II

46A: Ambassador, formerly mentioned under Rambler, was the top of the AMC range and was made available with a six-in-line and four V-8 power plants. Wheelbase and body size were unaltered.

46B: American Motors Corporation launched a small series of experimental models, a Coupé called AMX II, a 4-door Hardtop Cavalier and Vixen, a Sports model. Illustrated is the AMX II.

46C: Avanti II project was continued in South Bend, Indiana, where the complete car was built in small quantities after Studebaker had dropped the project. The moulded fibre-glass body was built on a strong frame as previously, and the power was provided by the Corvette 327 engine.

47A: **Buick's** Skylark was built on the same chassis as the Special series. It was fitted with the 6·6-litre 325-bhp engine as used in the Wildcat and Electra series. It came in three models, the one illustrated being the Hardtop Coupé, Model 44417E.

47B: Buick Skylark 4-door Hardtop, Model 44439E, came closest to the Buick Special 4-door Sedan, but was sportier and faster. It had no centre pillars.

47C: Buick Electra 225, Model 48439 BM, shared its chassis with the Wildcat and was one of the more luxurious Buick models. For 1966 a choice of 6·6- or 7-litre V-8 engines was offered.

47A Buick Skylark

47C Buick Electra 225 Hardtop Sedan

47B Buick Skylark 4-door Hardtop

47D Cadillac Fleetwood Brougham

47D: Cadillac Fleetwood Brougham Series 61 was a new addition to the range and had been available on special order only during the previous year. It shared the longer wheelbase with the Series 60 Fleetwood Sixty Special, but featured more luxurious appointments.

1966

48A: **Cadillac** de Ville Series 63 featured minor body changes for 1966. Cadillac offered one 345-bhp 7-litre V-8 engine and Turbo-Hydramatic transmission on all models.

48A Cadillac Coupé de Ville

48B Chevrolet Chevelle Malibu Sedan

48D Chevrolet Caprice Custom Sedan

48B: **Chevrolet** Chevelle Malibu, Model 13369, was an intermediate between the Chevy II and other regular Chevrolets. It featured a slightly modified body for 1966. There were five series, 16 models and a choice of two Sixes and five V-8s. There was a Super Sport Series 396 available with a 6·5-litre V-8 only.

48C: **Chevrolet** Impala Sport Sedan, Model 16339, was available with a 6-cylinder 157-bhp engine and with a choice of six V-8s. Four transmission types were offered. Power steering and power brakes were standard on some, and optional on other models.

48D: **Chevrolet** Caprice, Model 16647 CX, was the new top of the range model for Chevrolet. It was available with V-8 engines, power steering and power brakes. It had a similar chassis to the Biscayne, Bel-Air and Impala series.

48C Chevrolet Impala Sport Sedan

49A: **Chevrolet** Corvette Mako Shark was a fascinating styling study for future Corvette series, which for 1966 still offered the Stingray.

49A Chevrolet Corvette Mako Shark II

49B Chrysler 300 2-door Hardtop

49B: **Chrysler** 300, Model BC2-M, was based on the Newport series and sported luxury appointments with more power. Power-operated disc brakes were optional; a choice of 6·3- and 7·2-litre V-8 was available.

49C: **Dodge** Charger was a new model with sporty lines, like the Coronet series it was an intermediate size. The standard engine was a 5·2-litre 230-bhp V-8 unit with a two-barrel carb; a 6·5-litre engine was optional.

49D: **Dodge** Polara 4-door Hardtop was available only with a V-8 in the Polara 318 and Polara 500 series, with seven different models. A choice of four V-8 engines (except for Polara 318) and power front disc brakes was optional. The Monaco was similar in that it shared the same body unit as the Polara, offering two series and six models.

49C Dodge Charger

49D Dodge Polara 4-door Hardtop

1966

page 50

50A: Excalibur, the American 'replica' of the 1927–30 Mercedes-Benz SSK Sports Car, appeared to be a success. Powered by a 350 hp Corvette engine; with 4-speed manual or 3-speed automatic transmission. Disc brakes were standard.

50B: Ford's Experimental Department was testing public opinion towards yet another sporting machine, the Comet Escapade.

50C: Ford Falcon Futura Sports Coupé, Model 62C. New bodies with wheelbase increased by 1·5 in. for 1966, and choice of Sixes and V-8s. The Falcon range featured a total of 10 models in three series, plus a new Futura Sports Coupé illustrated here. Power brakes were available on Falcon.

50D: Ford Galaxie Station Wagon with new dual action tailgate, a standard feature on all Ford and Fairlane Wagons, and an option on Falcon Wagons.

50A Excalibur SS

50B Comet Escapade

50C Ford Falcon Futura

50D Ford Country Squire Station Wagon

page 51

1966

51A: **Ford** Mustang sold in Hardtop, Fastback and Convertible models. Top of the series was powerful Mustang Shelby 350 GT Street Version and 350 GT Competition. Top speeds attained were approximately 150 mph. Illustrated here is the Model 65A.

51B: **Ford** Prototype GT 40 was built for closed track and road racing. Designed and built in England, and powered by a 4·7-litre US V-8 unit, with 5-speed ZF transmission. Road version is illustrated here.

51C Imperial Crown

51C: **Imperial** Crown 4-door Hardtop (illustrated) and Le Baron Model BY1-H were the only two remaining series of the make. There were only minor changes to the body and chassis for 1966.

51D: **Lincoln** Continental for 1966 was 4·6 in. longer but retained the old 126 in. wheelbase. New for 1966 was the 2-door Hardtop, called the Continental Mark II Coupé, powered by a 462 CID V-8, with a 10% increase in performance.

51A Ford Mustang Hardtop

51B Ford GT 40

51D Lincoln Continental 4-door Sedan

1966

page 52

52A: Marlin, by AMC, had a number of styling and interior changes. A swaybar had been added to the Marlin Six for improved handling. Two Sixes and three V-8's were available, plus an option of four transmission types.

52B: Mercury Park Lane, Model 57F, settled among the top class USA cars for 1966. The Standard engine was a 330-bhp 410 CID. Transmissions were new and 12 lb lighter, due to use of aluminium die casting. Including the Comet there were 4 series, totalling 15 models.

52A Marlin Coupé

52B Mercury Park Lane 4-door Hardtop

52C: Oldsmobile Cutlass Holiday, Model 33839E, belonged to F85 series and featured two engine options: 5·4- and 6·5-litre V-8. The V-6 engine was dropped, being replaced by an in-line OHV Six, 250 CID 155 bhp.

52D: Oldsmobile Toronado took front-wheel drive back to America. It was available in only one body style—a 2-door Hardtop. One 425 CID 385-bhp engine with Turbo-Hydramatic transmission was fitted as a standard power pack, no options. The large overhang was necessary to accommodate the engine and to enable the use of a low bonnet and grille line.

52C Oldsmobile Cutlass Holiday Hardtop Sedan

52E: Plymouth Valiant Signet 200 Station Wagon, Model BV1-H, was one of five Valiants, which included Barracuda and Barracuda 'S', totalling 9 models. Three Sixes and four V-8's were available. The big Plymouth models comprised 14 series.

52E Plymouth Valiant Signet 200

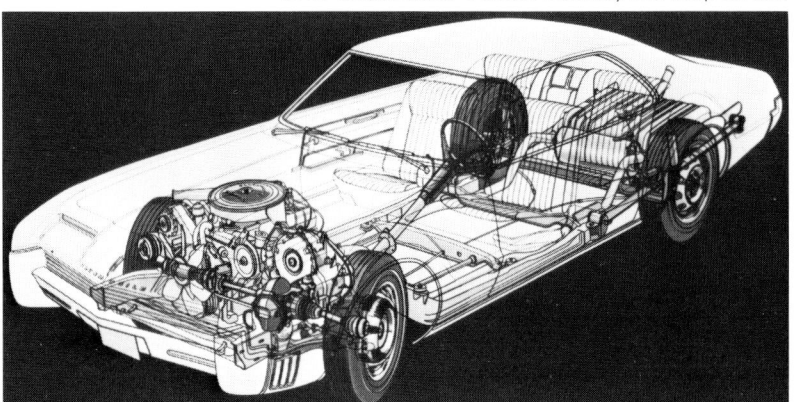

52D Oldsmobile Toronado

1966

53A Pontiac GTO

53B Pontiac Le Mans Sprint

53A: **Pontiac** GTO was a completely new series for 1966. Its 6·4-litre engine developed 335 bhp. The GTO was derived from the Tempest Le Mans series.

53B: **Pontiac** Tempest Le Mans Sprint was new for 1966 and featured a brand-new OHC Six in conjunction with a standard 4-speed gearbox.

53D: **Studebaker** finally stopped producing cars. There were only four series left, each with either a Six or a V-8 power plant, supplied by General Motors. Transmissions were 3-speed manual with or without overdrive or Flight-O-Matic automatic transmission. The series comprised Commander, Daytona, Cruiser and Wagonaire.

53C Rambler American Station Wagon

53C: **Rambler** American Station Wagon was one of three series: Six 220, 440 and Rogue. Standard power came from a 128-bhp 6-cylinder engine and 3-speed manual gearbox. Other series, including Rambler Renault Classic, totalled 9 models. Ambassador became a separate make.

53D Studebaker Cruiser 4-door Sedan

Wouldn't you know Hurst would introduce its new automatic control wrapped in a '67 GTO?

It's only proper. Hurst has been in GTO's since the first GTO was born. Now that they've kicked loose the Great One for '67, with a new engine, drive train components and a 3-speed Turbo-Hydramatic, Hurst is in there with something new of its own. A console-mounted Dual Gate control that's going to switch a lot of manual shift lovers over to automatic.

The reason is simple. Because the manual side of the Hurst automatic control is for *real*. This is no merchandising gimmick that promises you manual shift control, but in reality makes you guess your way through the automatic gears. The new Turbo-Hydro is a gutty, performance-prone transmission that's as at home on a race track as it is on the highway. And controlling it can be as precise as handling a fully synchronized manual transmission. The Dual Gate gives you that control with its positive latching mechanism that takes the guesswork out of gear-changing, going up or down. It eliminates any possibility of missing a gear, or accidentally hitting neutral and blowing an engine.

You're in complete control. You've got the automatic side when you feel shiftless and all the advantages of the manual side when you want to let it happen.

Soon you'll be able to buy Hurst automatic controls (along with all the other Hurst products) at your speed shop. Right now, though, you'll have to buy a Pontiac to get one. Write for details. Hurst Performance Products, Dept. 61B, Warminster, Pa. 18974.

1967 Rather alarming was yet another sharp decline in car sales for 1967 which totalled 8,377,000. American Motors Corporation faced a severe situation as their car sales dropped to a minimum (day production dropped from 1600 to 1100 units) due to the manufacturers' continuing compact car policy and capital shortage. The public obviously did not want compacts any more, thereby reducing the possibility of introducing new models at short notice. The market shares of the Big Three and AMC were approximately: General Motors 52%, Ford 28%, Chrysler 17% and AMC as little as 3%.

As for styling, quite clearly the fashionable hardtop body style, which included the fastback, was rapidly gaining popularity over the 2- and 4-door sedans. The Americans were in for a sporty image and were prepared to pay for that and for better quality. The Federal regulations on exhaust emissions passed Congress and were due to be enforced in the forthcoming year. This had an immediate effect on engine design in that the engineers had to reconsider basic combustion in the interests of low emissions. On the other hand a trend towards a generation of larger engine capacities was already noticeable since it was understood that emission control would mean a loss of power. The automatic transmission was back on the customer's list of favourite accessories after a sales slump in the early sixties. One of the first energy-absorbing steering-columns on the US market was fitted on the Chevrolet Corvair. Mercury introduced the Cougar and AMC replaced the Classic series by the Rebel series, which also became available as a Rambler Renault in certain European countries.

55A Ambassador 990 4-door Sedan

55C Buick Riviera

55A: **Ambassador** was AMC Rambler's top-of-the-line model. A new body, larger wheelbase, new rear axle and a choice of two Sixes and three V-8s. Front disc brakes optional in US and standard for some export markets. Three main series made eight models.

55B: **AMX** III followed sporty concept of AMX I and II prototypes of 1966. Fastback Station Wagon, still being a prototype, had different window treatments—one pillar on one side and none at all on the other. This was in answer to public demand. Wheelbase 109 in., length 189 in., luggage capacity 51 cu. ft.

55C: **Buick** Riviera, Model 49487 EN, 1966 body was virtually untouched for 1967. New and more powerful 7-litre V-8 engine drives the rear wheels of two versions, and three different axle ratios of 3·42:1, 3·91:1 and 3·07:1.

55B AMX III

1967

56A: Buick Le Sabre, Model 45439 E, was one of two series and seven models. It came with a standard 5·6-litre V-8, but a four-barrel carb version with 10·25:1 CR, adding an extra 40 bhp, was an available extra.

56B: Cadillac Eldorado was first front-drive Cadillac ever. It shared E-body with Toronado, but was longer and followed Toronado's technique of driving side-mounted transmission with a belt. Engine capacity 7 litres, output 340 hp.

56C: Cadillac Coupé de Ville Series Sixty, Model 68339 EG, was also available as Hardtop Sedan, Convertible and Sedan.

56D: Chevrolet Corvair Monza Sport Sedan, Model 10539 A, was one of four remaining bodies for 1967. Corsa was dropped, together with 140 bhp 4-carb and 180 bhp turbo-charged engines. Energy-absorbing steering-column was optional.

56E: Chevrolet Camaro Super Sport Coupé came as a late answer to Ford Mustang and the like. Two bodies, Hardtop and Convertible, two Sixes and three V-8s, 5·3 litres as Rallye Sport and 5·7 litres as Super Sport '350' were available. Four transmission types were offered. Note concealed headlamps.

56A Buick Le Sabre Four-door Hardtop

56B Cadillac Eldorado

56C Cadillac Coupé de Ville

56D Chevrolet Corvair Monza Sport Sedan

56E Chevrolet Camaro Super Sport Coupé

57A Chrysler New Yorker 4-door Hardtop

57B Dodge Dart GT

57C Dodge Coronet 500

57D Dodge Monaco

57E Dodge Polara 500

57A: Chrysler New Yorker, Model CC3-H, with detail changes for 1967. Available with two 7·2-litre V-8 engines of 350 and 375 bhp. Three models in New Yorker series.

57B: Dodge Dart, Model CL2-P, featured new body for 1967. Dart range consisted of 3 series: Dart, Dart 270 and Dart GT, and 6 models. Disc brakes at the front were optional for models sold in the US.

57C: Dodge Coronet 500 Hardtop, Model CL2-P, was luxury model of medium-sized Coronet range, consisting of 10 series and 25 models, including new Economy Station Wagon and new R/T series.

57D/E: Dodge Monaco and Polara were top of the line Dodges in 1967. Monaco was available in six models and Polara in nine. Wheelbase was same for both cars; five power plants were offered, V-8 only.

1967

58A Excalibur 35 X

58B Excalibur SS Roadster

58A: **Excalibur** was a USA firm, but type 35 X was constructed in Monte Carlo (France) and this particular model, featuring an Opel Commodore 2500 power plant, was a replica of the famous Bugatti of the thirties.

58B: **Excalibur** SS Roadster of Milwaukee factory featured 350-bhp Chevrolet Corvette power plant with one four-barrel carb. There were three models.

58C Ford Fairlane 500

58C: **Ford** Fairlane 500 Sedan, Model 54B, was basic model of medium-sized Fairlane range of four series and 13 models. Wheelbase 115·9 in. Choice of one Six and three 8-cylinder engines.

58D: **Ford** Mustang GT 350 and GT 500 were Shelby-modified versions with 4·7- and 7-litre 'Cobra' engines, respectively giving 306 and 380 bhp. Modified suspension and rollbar as standard fittings; lightweight body optional.

58D Ford Mustang GT 500

59A Ford Thunderbird 4-door Landau

59B Imperial Crown

59B: Imperial Crown Hardtop Sedan featured new unit construction body. There were 3 series: Imperial, Crown and Le Baron, and 5 models. All had automatic transmission and a 7·2-litre V-8 power plant (as for Chrysler New Yorker, with which it also shared body shell).

59A: Ford Thunderbird 4-door Landau, Model 57B, was first 4-door T-bird. It had a 2-in. longer wheelbase. Two V-8 engines were available in three models: Hardtop, Landau Hardtop and Landau. No manual transmission.

59C Kaiser Jeep 'Jeepster'

59D Kaiser Jeep Wagoneer

59C: Kaiser Jeepster and Jeepster Commando were new series of 4-wheel-drive Jeep models. Choice of 4 body styles and 2·2-litre 4-cylinder or 3·7-litre V-6. Three-speed manual or automatic transmission.
59D: Kaiser Jeep Wagoneer was a 4-wheel-drive model and available with standard new 145-bhp 'Hi-Torque' six-in-line engine and optional 250 bhp 'Vigilante' V-8. Turbo-Hydramatic automatic transmission, standard 3-speed or overdrive transmissions were offered with both engines.

1967
page 60

60A: Lincoln Continental Hardtop Coupé, Model 65A, featured small detail changes to body for 1967. 7·6-litre V-8 engine delivered 340 bhp.

60B: Marlin was AMC's sports model with new body, longer wheelbase and new rear suspension for 1967. Offered with 4 engine and 4 transmission options, including automatic transmission.

60C: Mercury Cougar, Model 65A, new for 1967 from Lincoln-Mercury Division. Cougar offered three power plants: 289 CID 200-bhp V-8 (also with a 225-bhp version) and a 390 CID 320-bhp V-8 for Cougar and Cougar XR-7 GT.

60D: Oldsmobile Delta 88, Model 35839 E, seen here with Miss America 1967, offered new lines and choice of four 7-litre V-8 engines. Three Delta and Delmont series comprised 10 models.

60E: Oldsmobile Toronado, Model 39687, with slightly modified body for 1967. One 385-bhp 7-litre engine and automatic transmission only, driving the front wheels.

60A Lincoln Continental Hardtop Coupé

60B Marlin Fastback Hardtop

60C Mercury Cougar

60D Oldsmobile Delta 88 Hardtop Sedan

60E Oldsmobile Toronado

61A: **Oldsmobile** Cutlass Supreme was top model of intermediate F85 Cutlass series and came with V-8 engine only. Cutlass Series consisted of 5 models and 3 engines.

61A Oldsmobile Cutlass Supreme Holiday

61B: **Plymouth** Valiant Signet, Model CV1-H. Sold as Valiant in some countries. New body and increased wheelbase for 1967. Choice of two Sixes and two V-8 engines. Torqueflite automatic transmission available.

61C: **Plymouth** Barracuda Formula GX 'Idea Car' was a variation on the then current Barracuda, with modified fastback styling. Body construction was of fibre-glass, 108 in. wheelbase. Front bumper formed integral part of the body.

61B Plymouth Valiant Signet

61D Pontiac GTO Cabriolet

61D: **Pontiac** GTO was sportiest model of a total of 35 models for 1967. It came with 400 CID four-barrel carb engine of 335 bhp. Second GM car with optional front disc brakes.

61C Plymouth Barracuda Formula GX 'Idea Car'

1967

page 62

62A Pontiac Le Mans

62B Pontiac Firebird

62B Pontiac Firebird

62A: **Pontiac** Le Mans Series Tempest, Model 23717 AT, featured in-line Six of 3·7 litres, 210 bhp as standard equipment. CR was 10·5:1. Tempest consisted of 4 series, totalling 14 models, out of which there were 4 Le Mans models.

62B: **Pontiac** Firebird was new for 1967 and shared the same 'F' body shell with Chevy's Camaro. Pontiac made Firebird available with 400 CID V-8 as in the GTO, but also with a range of six-in-line engines, starting with standard 1-barrel 230 CID 165 bhp OHC. 3- and 4-speed manual trans. were available as well as an optional 2-speed auto-trans. With 400 CID engine however auto. trans. was 3-speed Turbo-Hydramatic, and this model also featured heavy duty suspension and air scoops on the bonnet.

62D Rambler Renault Rebel

62C Rambler Rebel 770 Station Wagon

62C: **Rambler** Rebel replaced Classic series. New body with longer wheelbase; luxury model SST. Choice of two 6-cylinder and three V-8 engines. Three series (Rebel 550, 770 and SST) consisted of 8 models.

62D: **Rambler** Renault Rebel, CKD production through Régie Nationale des Usines Renault, in Haren, Belgium. Only one 3·8-litre 6-cylinder 155-bhp engine and two transmission options, one 4-door Sedan model only, front disc brakes as a standard fitting. Project stopped in 1967.

page 63

1968

US car sales had improved considerably in 1968, totalling 9,656,000 passenger cars, and with trucks included exceeded the 10 million mark. Also American Motors were reviving their financial structure and after the initial success of the Javelin, the even more advanced-looking AMX was introduced. Chevrolet's Corvair series were back to a one-model policy, while the existing Corvette got a completely new body. It was inspired by the Mako Shark prototype. Lincoln introduced a luxury short wheelbase Coupé model and called it the Mark III; it had distinctive styling with European front-end treatment. It came as a separate line to the existing Continental series.

Safety regulations were catching up, becoming stronger and more involved, for example, repositioning the petrol tank, the fitting of seat belts, revised door locks, dual-braking circuits and laminated windscreens, to name but a few. It was obvious that this was going to cost a tremendous amount of money, most of which had to be paid by the customer. US cars became more expensive and it seemed only fair that most of the regulations should apply to imported cars as well.

63A: **Ambassador** SST Sedan, AMC was one of seven models for 1968. New for 1968 was SST series shown here (also as 2-door Hardtop). Available with V-8 engines only.

63A Ambassador SST Sedan

63B/C: **AMX** II introduced early in 1968, complementing the already successful 4-seater Javelin. New 390 CID V-8 engine featuring highest displacement ever offered by AMC. Standard was 6-cylinder 290 CID and a 340 CID V-8 as first option. Unit body construction.

63D: **Buick** Skylark Custom 4-door Hardtop, Model 44439 JG, featured an all new body on an increased wb; 230-bhp V-8 was standard equipment.

63B AMX

63C AMX

63D Buick Skylark Custom

1968

page 64

64A Buick Electra 225 2-door Hardtop

64A: Buick Electra, Model 48439 JW, was based on Wildcat chassis but featured 430 CID V-8 engine and Super Turbine automatic transmission as standard equipment. Power brakes and power steering were also standard. Electra came in 7 models.

64C Cadillac Fleetwood Brougham

64B: Cadillac de Ville was available in 7 models. Shown here is the de Ville Convertible, Model 68349 IY. The other series were: Calais, Fleetwood Sixty, Brougham, Seventy-Five and Eldorado. For 1968 there was a bigger 7·7-litre V-8 power plant.

64C: Cadillac Fleetwood Brougham, Model 68169 JY, was one of 11 Cadillac models for 1968. Only Series 75 had longer wheelbases.

64D: Chevrolet Chevy II, Model 11327 (as shown here) was built on a longer 111 in. wheelbase and wider track for 1968. It also featured a new body styling. Chevy II, which came between Corvair and Chevelle, comprised only 2 models and was still available with a 4-cylinder engine.

64B Cadillac de Ville Convertible

64D Chevrolet Chevy II Nova Coupé

65A Chevrolet Caprice Coupé

65A: **Chevrolet** Caprice was top of Chevrolet line. Model 16647 HM, as shown here, was one of only 4 models. It came with a choice of 5 V-8 power plants and 5 transmissions.

65B: **Chevrolet** Corvette with complete new body for 1968. Also available as Coupé version with removable roof panels as an optional extra. Shown here is Convertible, Model 19467 FU.

65C Chrysler 300

65C: **Chrysler** 300, Model DC 2-M, was hardly changed for 1968. It featured retractable headlamps and a new roof line. Now with automatic transmission only.

65D: **Dodge** Coronet series had a new body for 1968, was slightly larger and comprised six models. Choice of 6 cylinders and V-8's.

65B Chevrolet Corvette Stingray

65D Dodge Coronet

1968

66A Dodge Polara

66A: Dodge Polara was top of the line series and featured detail changes and a slightly changed roof line. Polara and Monaco series totalled 14 models, plus a choice of five V-8 engine varieties and three transmissions.

66B Dodge Charger III

66C Dodge Charger III

66B/C: Dodge Charger III was an experimental car built by Chrysler's Dodge division. This 2-seater was only 42 in. high, 184 in. long and 73 in. wide. No doors but jet-aircraft-type canopy swinging open, with steering-wheel instrument cluster pad moving up while seats elevate to admit passengers.

66D: Ford Falcon Futura featured detail changes front and rear. Front disc brakes optional, manual 3-speed synchromesh gearbox as standard along with 6- and 8-cylinder engine options. Four-speed manual transmission available in conjunction with 4·7- and 4·9-litre engines only. Automatic transmission available on all models.

66D Ford Falcon Futura Sports Coupé

1968

67A: **Ford** Fairlane Torino was the new, sporty line in Fairlane series. Fairlane series comprised 15 models of which six were Torino and Torino GT Models. 6- and 8-cylinder engines and automatic transmission available.

67B: **Ford** LTD was based on Galaxie series. Custom and Custom 500, Galaxie 500, XL, LTD and Station Wagon totalled 21 models, of which only three were LTD's. New roof line and detail changes only.

67A Ford Fairlane Torino GT Fastback

67C Imperial Crown Hardtop Sedan

67D Javelin SST

67B Ford LTD Hardtop

67C: **Imperial** Crown and Le Baron were the only two series that remained for 1968. Crown came in 4 models, Le Baron in only one. There was one 7·2-litre 350-bhp V-8 and one automatic transmission, Torqueflite Eight.

67D: **Javelin** SST was new sporty AMC model for 1968. It came in two guises: Javelin and Javelin SST as shown. Choice of a 3·8-litre six-in-line and three V-8 engines of 4·7-litre 225 bhp and 5·6-litre 280 bhp. Manual 3-speed and automatic transmission on 6-cylinder models; 4-speed manual in conjunction with 200, 225 and 280 bhp. Auto. trans. not available on 225 bhp. Front disc brakes optional on V-8 models.

1968

68A Kaiser Jeep Gladiator

68B Lincoln Continental Mk III Coupé

68C Mercury Montego MX

68D Mercury Cyclone GT Hardtop

68A: Kaiser Jeep Gladiator shown here with camper package was built on 126-in. wheelbase J-3000 Gladiator with equipment including heavy duty rear axles, springs, tyres and wheels.

68B: Lincoln Continental Mk III was new luxury Coupé on separate chassis and shorter wheelbase. It used smaller V-8 engine than Sedan, but with higher power output, i.e. 370 bhp. Automatic transmission only.

68C: Mercury Montego, Montego MX and Montego Brougham were new for 1968. Eight models with engines ranging from 3·3-litre six-in-line to 7-litre V-8. Same wheelbase as Cyclone series. Shown here is Montego MX 2-door Hardtop.

68D: Mercury Cyclone GT Hardtop Fastback. Sportiest version of Montego and Cyclone series. Four models with new body for 1968. Choice of two 4·9-litre and one 6·4-litre engine for Cyclone. 6·4-litre Standard 340 bhp for Cyclone GT. Manual 3- and 4-speed transmissions only for Cyclone GT.

69A Oldsmobile 442 Coupé Fastback

69A: Oldsmobile 442 was luxury model on swb chassis of F85 series. There were 2 Coupés and 1 Convertible, and a choice of nine engine and transmission options.

69B: Oldsmobile Cutlass featured detail changes and a new roof line for 1968. It shared technical specifications with F85 and comprised 12 models including Convertibles and Station Wagons. There were three 6-cylinder engine and transmission options and five V-8 engine and transmission varieties.

69C Plymouth Barracuda S

69C: Plymouth Barracuda Notchback, Model DB2-H, had changed very little for 1968. Shown here is Barracuda S which featured new 5·6-litre V-8 as standard equipment. Front disc brakes standard with 6·5-litre engine.

69D: Plymouth Fury III, Model DP2-M, was largest of Plymouth line. It offered a choice of five V-8 engines between 5·2- and 7·2-litres. There were 10 Fury Series with V-8 engine totalling 19 models. V-8 Fury Six consisted of 5 series with 8 models. Standard engine was 5·2 litres 233 bhp.

69B Oldsmobile Cutlass

69D Plymouth Fury III

1968

70A Pontiac Le Mans 4-door Hardtop

70B Pontiac Bonneville Convertible

70C Rambler American 440 Station Wagon

70D Rambler Rogue Hardtop

70A: **Pontiac** Le Mans, Model 23737 KS, featured standard 6-cylinder 175-bhp engine with manual 3-speed trans. 'Tempest Torque' was optional. Le Mans series comprised 4 models. For the first time 2-door models had shorter wheelbase.

70B: **Pontiac** Bonneville represented top of the line series. Convertible shown was one of 4 models. Standard engine and transmission were 6·6-litre 345-bhp V-8, whereas 7-litre 390-bhp engine was offered with a four-barrel carb. and 10·75:1 CR.

70C/D: **Rambler** American was divided into three series: Standard, 440 and Rogue. 440 Station Wagon as shown was available with 3·3-litre six-cylinder in-line engine (not available for Rogue which featured standard 6-cylinder engine of 3·8-litre. In all there were two Sixes and two V-Eights. American series totalled 5 models only.

1969 Car sales for 1969 were slightly down at 9,583,000 vehicles. In fact this was only the forerunner of a much more dramatic decline in the year that was to follow. Amidst all the safety and emission regulations of the previous two years, the US car industry enjoyed the relaxation of the exhaust emission until 1970 or maybe even 1971. Safety was still the word for 1969 though things were calming down a bit.

A lot of changes were introduced among which were the Pontiac with the longest-ever nose, the Grand Prix, new bodies for Mustang and Cougar, while General Motors introduced the side impact rail in the doors as a standard item on most of its cars. Axle ratio extremes in 1969 ranged from 2·56:1 (Oldsmobile) to something as high as 5·00:1 on the AMX. Ford and Chrysler introduced new limited slip differentials and a big multiple-disc clutch pack with high-angle pre-loaded cone clutches.

Through-flow ventilation became the word for 1969, explaining the disappearing front quarter vent windows which made way for ventilation outlets on the facia. Radio aerials in the front window's glass and heated rear windows had become fashionable, and such expensive accessories as electric sliding roof and speed control were selling very well. The compact had almost been forgotten; it was the intermediate model range that held the designer's attention. European import sales were still booming though.

71B Ambassador SST Station Wagon

71A Ambassador SST 4-door Sedan

71A: **Ambassador** SST was AMC's prestige model under a separate name. The Ambassador line featured 6 models with many detail changes to front and rear for 1969. Wheelbase and overall length were increased 4 in. and the track widened to 60 in. Choice of one Six and four V-eight engines, though 6-cylinder engine was not available for SST models, which had standard 4·7-litre 200-bhp V-8 power plant.
71B: **Ambassador** and Rebel (another AMC Rambler line) offered their Station Wagon series with 'Dual-Swing' tailgate. Fitted with standard power plant of 4·7 litres V-8 coupled with automatic transmission only.
71C: **AMX** was American Motors' sportiest model, which featured a standard V8, four barrel, 290 CID engine, with 343 and 390 CID four-barrel V-8's optional. Though basically a 2-seater, AMX was longer and also had a longer wheelbase than the 4-seater Javelin.

71C AMX Hardtop Fastback Coupé

1969

72A: **Avanti** II was still produced after Studebaker as a make had ceased to exist. Raymond Loewy's design was little changed for 1969. Power unit was 300-bhp V-8 Chevrolet engine. Front wheel disc brakes as standard equipment. Choice of manual 4-speed and Borg Warner automatic transmission.

72A Avanti II

72B: **Buick** Skylark HZ Custom Convertible, Model 44467, was available with V-8 power plant only. Standard engine was 5·7-litre 230-bhp V-8. Transmission options were manual 3-speed and Turbo-Hydramatic 350. Series Six Special de Luxe, Skylark, V-8 Special de Luxe, Skylark Custom and Sports Wagon comprised four 6-cylinder and seven V-8 engined models. Detail changes front and rear for 1969.

72C: **Buick** Wildcat Custom V-8 Hardtop Coupé was based on Le Sabre chassis and shared Le Sabre's body shell, representing the sportier models. Shorter wheelbase as well as detail changes on front suspension. Wildcat came in 2 series and 6 models, standard engine being 7-litre 360-bhp V-8.

72D: **Buick** Riviera, Model 49487, featured no changes for 1969. Standard engine was 7-litre 360-bhp V-8 as in Wildcat and Electra models. Automatic transmission. Turbo-Hydramatic 400 as standard equipment, anti-slip differential and variable power steering optional.

72B Buick Skylark Custom Convertible

72C Buick Wildcat Custom V-8 Hardtop Coupé

72E: **Cadillac** de Ville Convertible was one of 4 de Ville models. Disc brakes were now standard equipment on all Series. Only one power plant and transmission type was available for all 6 series and 10 models (of which the Fleetwood 75 Limousine was still the largest). Some detail changes on front and rear end for 1969.

72F: **Cadillac** Fleetwood Eldorado, Model 69347 EG, was available in only one model. It was Cadillac's only front-drive car, and one of two in the American industry, the other one being the Oldsmobile Toronado. It featured the same 7·7-litre 375-bhp V-8 engine as the other Cadillacs. Cadillac still built a separate chassis and a heavy live rear axle.

72D Buick Riviera

72E Cadillac de Ville Convertible

72F Cadillac Fleetwood Eldorado

73A Chevrolet Corvair Monza

73B Chevrolet Chevelle Malibu 350

73C Chevrolet Camaro 'RS' Convertible

73A: **Chevrolet** Corvair Monza had featured only one 2-door model since 1968. In 1969 incidentally, Corvair lost the battle against Ralph Nader and was taken out of production. Engine options apart from 2·7-litre 95-bhp 2 carb. power plant were 112 bhp with raised CR from 8·25 to 9·25:1 and 142-bhp 4 carb. version.

73B: **Chevrolet** Chevelle Malibu 350, Model 13539 B, was available in a slightly reduced number of models for 1969. Chevelle came between Nova and regular-sized models, which offered 5 series and 15 models. Standard engine was 3·8-litre 6-cylinder 140-bhp; standard engine for V-8 series was 5-litre 200-bhp V-8. Chevelle featured 5 series and 15 models, 8 of which were Station Wagons.

73C: **Chevrolet** Camaro 'RS' Convertible featured standard 350 CID V-8 and power output up to 325 bhp on the various options. Power disc brakes were standard equipment, while Hurst-linkage 4-speed transmission was available as an extra. Rally-Sport and (SS) Super Sport featured wider 7-in. wheel rims. Standard Camaro engine (not for RS models) was 3·8-litre, 6-cylinder 140-bhp.

73D: **Chrysler** 300, Model EC2-M, was also available as a 4-door Sedan Hardtop and as a Convertible. Completely new and longer bodies for 1969. Standard engine for 300 and New Yorker Series was 7·2-litre 350-bhp V-8. Other series were Newport, Newport Custom and Town & Country Station Wagons, totalling 15 models. Standard engine (not for 300 models) was 6·3-litre 290-bhp V-8.

73E: **Dodge** Dart Swinger, Model EL2P, was new Dart series for 1969. Available in only one Coupé Hardtop model it offered Six and V-8 engines, 3 and 4-speed manual and 3-speed automatic transmission.

73D Chrysler 300 Hardtop

73E Dodge Dart Swinger

1969

74A Dodge Monaco Sedan Hardtop

74A: Dodge Monaco was top model range for Dodge in 1969. It was offered in 5 models including a Station Wagon. Shown here is Sedan Hardtop, Model ED 2-H. Standard engine was 6·3-litre 290-bhp V-8 with choice of 3-speed manual or 3-speed automatic transmission.

74B: Dodge Charger, Model EX2-P showed little change for 1969. Charger was available in 2 series and 2 models: Charger and Charger RH. Standard engine for Charger was 5·2-litre V-8 developing 230 bhp, and standard engine for Charger R/T was 7·2-litre 375-bhp V-8. Transmission options were either a 3-speed manual and a Torqueflite automatic transmission for Charger and a 4-speed manual or Torqueflite automatic transmission for R/T.

74C: Ford Fairlane Torino 4-door Sedan, Model 54C, was luxury series based on Fairlane. It featured a unit body construction. Engine options were 4·1-litre six, 4·9-litre V-8, 5·8-litre V-8, 5·8-litre V-8 290 bhp, 6·4-litre V-8 320 bhp. Ford Fairlane (to which belonged also series Fairlane 500, Torino, Torino GT and Cobra) amounted to 22 models.

74D: Ford Mustang, Model 65A 2-door Hardtop featured a new body for 1969. Standard engine was 3·3-litre six-in-line 115 bhp, while the biggest engine was a 7-litre V-8, developing 335 bhp. Mustang Shelby GT 350+500 offered 5·8- and 7-litre V-8 engines, which developed 290 and 335 bhp respectively. Apart from Shelby series there were 5 series and 11 Mustang models.

74E: Ford Thunderbird Landau 2-door Hardtop featured minor detail changes for 1969. Six models included 4-door Landau. There was only one engine-transmission option, i.e. 7-litre 360-bhp V-8 and 'Select-Shift' automatic transmission.

74C Ford Fairlane Torino

74D Ford Mustang

74B Dodge Charger

74E Ford Thunderbird Landau

page 74

1969

75A Imperial Le Baron Hardtop Sedan

75B Javelin SST

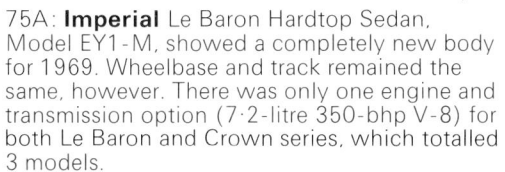

75A: **Imperial** Le Baron Hardtop Sedan, Model EY1-M, showed a completely new body for 1969. Wheelbase and track remained the same, however. There was only one engine and transmission option (7·2-litre 350-bhp V-8) for both Le Baron and Crown series, which totalled 3 models.

75B: **Javelin** SST offered one 232 CID 6-cylinder and an optional 290 CID two barrel V-8. The floor-mounted 3-speed manual transmission as standard equipment was new, and there were minor detail changes. 3-speed automatic transmission was also available. CKD assembly of both Javelin and AMX was started at Wilhelm Karmann G.m.b.H. in West Germany for European market. Mag-type wheels (pictured) were an option.

75C: **Lincoln** Continental Mark III, Model 65A, was appreciably smaller than Lincoln Continental Sedan and came only as a 2-door Hardtop version. 7·5-litre engine and automatic transmission were same as for Continental Sedans. Power disc brakes at the front were a standard feature.

75D: **Lincoln** Continental built the Sedan and Hardtop with a new front grille and detail changes. More powerful V-8 engine and longer body.

75E: **Mercury** Comet featured new body for 1969. It shared body shell and mechanics with Montego and Cyclone series. Comet came in 2-door Sports Coupé only and standard engine was 4·1-litre 155-bhp 6-cylinder in-line. Comet production, one time Mercury compact model, was phased out in 1969.

75C Lincoln Continental Mk III

75D Lincoln Continental Sedan

75E Mercury Comet Sports Coupé

1969

76A Mercury Cougar Convertible

76B Mercury Brougham 4-door Hardtop

76A: Mercury Cougar, Model 65A, was one of two models, the other being the Cougar XR 7. There were 5 options. Standard engine was 5·8-litre 250-bhp V-8 (as used in Comet and Montego series). 6·4-litre 320-bhp and 7-litre 335-bhp V-8's were alternative power plants.

76B: Mercury Brougham featured a body shell that was shared with Marquis and new Marauder series. It came in Sedan, Sedan Hardtop and 2-door Coupé Hardtop versions with 7-litre 320-bhp V-8 standard engine. Auto. trans. only.

76C: Oldsmobile Cutlass Holiday Hardtop Sedan, Model 34239 HZ, was hardly changed for 1969 except for the new Turbo-Hydramatic auto. trans. There were two standard engines, one 6 and one V-8 of 4·1 litre 155 bhp and 5·7 litre 250 bhp respectively. Standard transmission was 3-speed, manual, column-shift with 4-speed manual and automatic transmission as options.

76D Oldsmobile Ninety-Eight

76C Oldsmobile Cutlass Sedan

76D: Oldsmobile Ninety-Eight, Model 38639 JY, was Olds's luxury model which featured a new body and longer wheelbase for 1969. Front wheel disc brakes were standard equipment on export models. Basic engine/transmission was 7·4 litre 365 bhp with Turbo-Hydramatic.

77A Oldsmobile Toronado

77B Plymouth Valiant Signet Sedan

77D Plymouth GTX

77C Plymouth Barracuda

77A: Oldsmobile Toronado, Model 39487 JW, was hardly changed for 1969 except for a slightly longer trunk. Same 375- and 400-bhp engines as in previous year and Turbo-Hydramatic auto. trans. only.

77B: Plymouth Valiant Signet Sedan, Model EV1-L, offered choice of two 6-cylinder and two V-8 engines in an only slightly modified body. Standard transmission was manual 3-speed column gear change with synchromesh on 2nd and 3rd; automatic 'Torque Flite' transmission was also available. Valiant offered two series: 100 Six and V-8 and Signet Six and V-8 with two models each.

77C: Plymouth Barracuda EB1-H was based on Valiant models but featured more powerful engines except for the basic 3·7-litre 145-bhp six-in-line. Most powerful was 6·3-litre 330-bhp V-8 for Barracuda 'S' and 'Cuda' which also featured a standard manual 4-speed transmission. Barracuda was available in 4 models, including a Convertible, and offered a choice of 7 power/transmission options.

77D: Plymouth GTX 2-door Hardtop series, together with Belvedere V-8, Road Runner, Satellite, Sport Satellite and GTX, amounted to 18 models and 9 engine/transmission options. Standard engine/transmission for GTX was 7·2-litre 375-bhp V-8 with four-barrel carb. Anti-slip differential was used in conjunction with both 7- and 7·2-litre power plants.

1969

78A Pontiac Le Mans 4-door Hardtop

78B Pontiac Firebird

78A: Pontiac Le Mans, Model 23737 PU, was fastest of Tempest series, which comprised Tempest, Tempest Custom S, Le Mans and Le Mans Safari, totalling 13 models. Standard engine/transmission option was 4·1-litre 175-bhp six-in-line and manual 3-speed transmission. Detail changes for 1969 only.

78B: Pontiac Firebird, Model 22337 PY, featured a new body with an integral front bumper. Firebird was available as Hardtop Coupé and Convertible with a standard engine of 4·1-litre 175-bhp six-in-line. Other power options were 4·1 litre six-in-line 230 bhp, 5·8 litre 265 bhp and 325 bhp, 6·6 litre 330 bhp, 335 bhp and 345 bhp. There were 6 transmission options: 2 manual 3-speed, 2 manual 4-speed and 2 auto. trans. including the new Turbo-Hydramatic.

78C: Pontiac Grand Prix with new, shorter body on Catalina base. For 1969 Grand Prix featured longest hood in GM production history. There were 7 power/transmission options including manual 3- and 4-speed and automatic transmission.

78D/E: Pontiac Design principle and road-going town car of Pontiac division's efforts on steam engines.

78C Pontiac Grand Prix Coupé

78D Pontiac Steam Car

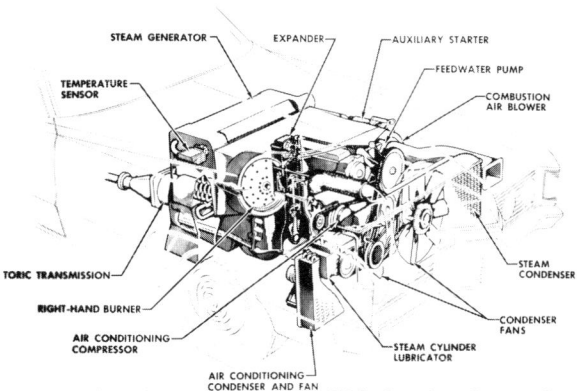

78E Pontiac Steam Car

1969

79A Rambler 440 Sedan

79B Rambler Rogue 2-door Hardtop

79C Rebel 4-door Sedan

79A: Rambler 440 Sedan (formerly American), like AMX and Javelin, was built in both the USA and at Wilhelm Karmann's assembly plant in West Germany. In the latter case special paint and interior treatment was added to give a European flair. The 440 Sedan featured a 232 CID 155-bhp six-in-line engine as standard.

79B: Rambler Rogue (formerly American) is top of the line of the small car series of AMC's Rambler. It featured a standard 3·8-litre 145-bhp six-in-line and a special 4·7-litre 225-bhp V-8, the latter with manual 4-speed only.

79C: **Rebel** was available as a 4-door Sedan, a 2-door Coupé Hardtop and a 5-door Station Wagon; in two versions, Standard and SST. Basic engine was 232 CID, 145-bhp six-in-line.

79D/E: **Rebel** 2-door Hardtop featured new rear-end styling, while SST models also featured stainless side trim strips and, on the 2-door Hardtop model, simulated louvres forward of the rear wheel opening. Biggest power plant for SST series was 280-bhp 5·6-litre V-8 in conjunction with automatic transmission only.

79D Rebel 2-door Hardtop

79E Rebel SST 2-door Hardtop

MAJOR AMERICAN CAR MAKES, 1960–1969

AMERICAN MOTORS GROUP
Ambassador	(from 1965)
AMX	(1968–71)
Javelin	(1968–75)
Marlin	(1965–68)
Metropolitan	(1960–62)
Rambler	(from 1956)
Rambler Renault	(1963–67)
Rebel	(1968–71)

CHRYSLER GROUP
Chrysler	(from 1923)
DeSoto	(1928–61)
Dodge	(from 1914)
Imperial	(from 1926)
Plymouth	(from 1928)

FORD GROUP
Ford	(from 1903)
Lincoln	(from 1920)
Mercury	(from 1938)
Meteor (Canada)	(1948–61)
Monarch (Canada)	(1946–61)

GENERAL MOTORS GROUP
Buick	(from 1903)
Cadillac	(from 1903)
Chevrolet	(from 1911)
Oldsmobile	(from 1896)
Pontiac	(from 1926)

OTHER MAKES
Avanti II	(from 1966)
Checker	(from 1921)
Cord	(1965–66)
Excalibur	(from 1965)
Kaiser Jeep	(1963–70)
Studebaker	(1902–66)
Willys (Overland)	(1908–63)

ACKNOWLEDGEMENTS

This book was compiled and written largely from historic source material in the library of the Olyslager Organisation. Additional photographs were kindly provided by American Motors, Chrysler, Ford and General Motors.

INDEX

Ambassador 9, 15, 55, 63, 71
American Motors 7, 8, 9, 10, 15, 16, 22, 29, 30, 36, 44, 45, 46, 52, 53, 55, 60, 62, 63, 67, 70, 71, 75, 79
AMX 46, 55, 63, 71
Avanti II 46, 72

Buick 4, 10, 16, 23, 30, 38, 46, 47, 55, 56, 63, 64, 72

Cadillac 4, 10, 16, 23, 30, 38, 39, 47, 48, 56, 64, 72
Checker 24, 31
Chevrolet 4, 5, 7, 8, 11, 16, 17, 23, 24, 25, 30, 31, 38, 39, 48, 49, 55, 56, 58, 62, 63, 64, 65, 72, 73
Chrysler 4, 5, 6, 11, 12, 16, 17, 18, 19, 25, 30, 31, 38, 40, 42, 49, 55, 57, 59, 65, 71, 73
Comet 7, 10, 20, 33, 50, 75
Continental 6, 10, 16, 28, 42, 51, 60, 63, 68, 75
Cord 40
Corvair 4, 5, 6, 11, 17, 24, 25, 30, 31, 39, 40, 55, 56, 63, 64, 73
Corvette 4, 5, 17, 25, 39, 41, 46, 49, 50, 58, 63, 65

Dart 5, 12, 16, 18, 21, 25, 30, 57, 73
DeSoto 5, 10, 12
Dodge 5, 10, 12, 16, 18, 21, 25, 26, 30, 32, 40, 46, 49, 57, 65, 66, 73, 74

Excalibur 41, 50, 58

Falcon 4, 6, 7, 18, 26, 27, 32, 50, 66
Ford 4, 6, 10, 12, 16, 18, 19, 26, 27, 30, 32, 41, 42, 50, 51, 55, 58, 59, 66, 67, 71, 74

General Motors 4, 10, 16, 30, 55, 71

Imperial 6, 13, 19, 28, 33, 42, 51, 59, 67, 75

Javelin 63, 67, 71, 75

Kaiser Jeep 59, 68

Lincoln 6, 13, 19, 28, 42, 51, 60, 63, 68, 75

Marlin 45, 52, 60
Mercury 7, 10, 13, 20, 23, 28, 33, 34, 42, 43, 52, 55, 60, 68, 75, 76
Metropolitan 7
Mustang 27, 30, 33, 41, 45, 51, 58, 71, 74

Oldsmobile 7, 10, 13, 14, 20, 28, 30, 34, 38, 43, 46, 52, 60, 61, 69, 71, 76, 77

Plymouth 7, 14, 20, 21, 29, 30, 35, 38, 44, 46, 53, 61, 62, 70, 71, 78

Rambler 8, 9, 22, 29, 30, 36, 44, 45, 46, 53, 62, 70, 79
Rambler Renault 22, 53, 55, 62
Rebel 62, 79

Stingray 23, 25, 49, 65
Studebaker 9, 15, 22, 23, 29, 30, 36, 37, 41, 45, 46, 53, 72

Tempest 10, 21, 29, 30, 44, 46, 62, 78
Thunderbird 6, 10, 12, 13, 19, 27, 41, 59, 74

Valiant 4, 5, 6, 11, 12, 20, 29, 35, 43, 44, 52, 61, 77

Willys 28

page 80